THE
RELUCTANT
ARTIST

The Reluctant Artist is for anyone who's thinking about becoming an artist as well as for those who are already in the thick of their work. Karen beautifully articulates what often isn't taught in most formal schools of art or even professional work settings, but should be. The wisdom and insights she offers are as essential as the tools and techniques of any creative craft. She left me with an even greater understanding of my own creative process, answering questions I'd always thought about but never considered to ask. This is a book that I intend to return to time and again for encouragement, guidance, and support.
–Diahann Reyes-Lane, *writer*

Choosing the life of an artist is never a simple decision, as it is often not the easy or stable path. Karen illustrates the repeated need to recommit to a vocational calling that is non-linear and operates in ebbs and flows. Though each artist's process varies, Karen reassuringly illustrates commonalities in which most artists can see themselves, offering encouragement to stay the course with greater confidence.
–Krista Machovina, *visual artist and curator*

Karen beautifully navigates the life and soul of an artist. Through self-reflection, authenticity, and a twist of spirituality, she overcomes the hardships of both life and the creative pursuit. Her wise perspective as a true artist is a reminder that you too can enjoy the creative dream and lifestyle.
–Evan Meyer, *founder of Beautify Earth*

In *The Reluctant Artist*, Karen Kinney does not simply present a how-to manual for being an artist. Instead, she weaves insightful vignettes about creativity and the creative process into a richly colored tapestry of inspiration for any aspiring artist.
–**Melanie Sklarz**, *creativity blogger, DoseofCreativity.com*

This book is an insightful companion for all artists. For any creative people who are questioning, seeking, changing direction or becoming more authentic, free, open, and influential, Karen's keen observations are refreshing and affirming. She provides a deeper understanding of the artist as individual and in community and also offers a broad look at the value and role of art in society. This is a book to read again and again, to share and discuss with others, and to gift to any burgeoning creative souls for nourishment and guidance along their journey.
–**Casey Robards**, *collaborative pianist, faculty, Central Michigan University*

We live in a time of self-definition. This is both a blessing and a curse: A blessing because more people can follow their dreams, and less so, because many know what they want, but not how to get there. Karen Kinney gives valuable direction, deep insight, and wise counsel to anyone pursuing art as a profession.
–**David Sandum**, *painter, philanthropist, author of I'll Run Till the Sun Goes Down*

This groundbreaking book gives permission to every artist to honor the creative space of their self-expression. In this personal account of creative ebbs and flows, joys and reluctance, and the balance of responsibility, I found comfort knowing that there are others who struggle with the constant pull between the heart, the mind, and reality. This book is a 'must read' for every person who is wondering how their own creative expression will impact the world. Bravo to Karen for providing the reasons for us all to dive in and find the deeper meaning in our lives and in the joy of self-expression!

–**Mary Campagna**, *visual artist, owner of Studio Collette*

THE
RELUCTANT
ARTIST

Navigating and Sustaining a Creative Path

KAREN KINNEY

Winged Bird Press
Los Angeles

The Reluctant Artist

Copyright ©2017 by Karen Kinney

Published by Winged Bird Press. Los Angeles, CA.

All rights reserved. This book or any portion thereof may not be reproduced or used in any manner whatsoever without the express written permission of the publisher, except for the use of brief quotations in a book review.

www.karenkinney.com

ISBN-10: 0-9989395-0-1
ISBN-13: 978-0-9989395-0-6

Cover art and design by Karen Kinney
Author photograph by Elizabeth Balch

First Printing, 2017

Printed in the United States of America

True success in the arts could be summed up by a simple refusal to give up. Our part is to just be faithful, to return and try again.

CONTENTS

Introduction 1

1 The Idea of Becoming 5
2 The Value of Art in Society 13
3 Creative Work and Its Distinctiveness 21
4 Allowing Your Truest Self to Come Forth 27
5 Freedom and Keeping an Open Mind 37
6 Encouragement 43
7 Being Misunderstood 49
8 Creating When You Don't Feel Like It 57
9 Commerce 67
10 The Ebb and Flow 75
11 Spirituality and Art 81
12 Listening and Being Comfortable with the Unknown .. 87
13 Replenishing the Well 93
14 Remembering That Artists Are Changemakers 99
15 Redemption in Life Calling 107

Introduction

The Reluctant Artist is perhaps an unexpected title for a book, I admit, especially in this day and age of grandiose-sounding sentiments like "Seize your dreams!" and reassurances that "The world is your oyster." But when this title popped into my head (long before the book was ever written), something about it rang true deep inside.

It is important to clarify up front that my use of the word "reluctant" does not mean wishing you were on a different path, as one might initially assume. Instead, it signifies recognition that the path you are called to is not the easiest path available. Most people who follow their true life calling can likely attest to this. There are numerous other directions they could have pursued that would have been simpler and required less from them. And, at the same time, these easier alternative routes would have been less rewarding and left them living a fraction of the life they could have lived. To follow your true life's work and the higher purpose beckoning to you requires a degree of sacrifice. Because we are creatures who gravitate toward comfort and ease, feeling some reluctance at points along the way is a normal human reaction if you are earnestly pursuing a calling. Overcoming this reluctance is part of the game.

The love of art, in a broader cultural sense, was not fostered in me to a great degree in my upbringing. I was an extremely creative child and enjoyed many personal outlets for creative expression throughout my youth, but art and culture as larger entities were not a big part of my childhood experience. So historically, I've never been one to seek out art museums or get into conversations about the meaning behind a particular sculpture or painting, etc. As a result, envisioning myself as an artist contributing to culture on a larger scale was not an inherent inclination. Furthermore, I am a private person (and was actually rather shy as a small child). Growing up, I loved music and played the piano for years, but recitals always produced feelings of dread. Performing in front of an audience was never something I looked forward to. Putting myself out there in the world to be seen (which of course one must also do as a visual artist) was not an innate impulse.

But despite these things, life has a funny way of moving us toward our calling and I was no exception. Over time, my path started to slowly lead me toward the work I was meant to do. Clues, experimentation, and trial and error eventually led to a deep awareness of the artist identity I'd had within me all along. It became clear on the road of self-discovery that not only did I find great joy in acts of creation, but that art and writing were also a large part of the destiny I was being called to. Not only did living this out fit with many of my gifts, but it became quite apparent that it would also bring tremendous value to the world around me. The stakes for not creating became higher than the stakes required to create. So, courage became my companion, and I set out on a journey that is still unfolding today. Although the word "reluctant" may acknowledge the struggle, I have also found deep life and freedom in becoming the creative individual I am meant to be. It is in honor of this that I pursue the artist's path.

— O N E —

The Idea of Becoming

This book is for those of you who sense a creative calling but have not yet found the courage to pursue it, and also for those of you who are well-established on your creative path and are looking for some sustenance and revitalization along the way. It may also be helpful for those who have experienced creative burnout and would like to begin anew, but feel unsure where to start. Essentially, it is for anyone who has something creative to express and could use some inspiration in their endeavors. It is written primarily from my own experience in the world of fine art making, although I've also dabbled in interior design, set design, decorative painting, and a few other creative fields. Mixed media art eventually surfaced as my true passion and became the place from which I've explored creativity in depth.

The focus of this book is not so much about the history that led up to my becoming an artist—meaning the journey that preceded my art career, or even more recently, the process that preceded the writing of this book—as it is on what I have learned about creativity since firmly committing myself to living it out. However, the process of becoming that paves the way for the definitive ownership of any identity is certainly a vital one, and I would be remiss to not mention its importance.

The truth is, I've always been more interested in the concept of becoming than in the accolades that follow once you establish yourself on a particular path. Although accolades are certainly fun and offer their fair share of motivation, I've found the excitement they generate wears off quickly. I really believe that allowing yourself to evolve in life is much more important than where you end up on any given spectrum.

In answering questions like "How do you define your success as an artist?", I think the most valuable and noteworthy thing is having allowed the artistry in the first place. Both claiming the identity of "artist" and expressing it to the world is a significant victory. Those of us whose parents were artists, or who have never struggled with the idea of needing to allow creativity are the exception, in my experience. The rest of us have huge battles to wage before even beginning. Cultural expectations, career pressures, and fear of failure are all common areas of struggle, to name a few. Overcoming these initial obstacles seems like more of a victory, in a fundamental sense, than any achievement that comes after. Not that achievements later aren't noteworthy or without struggle, by any means. But in my experience, they occur on a different battlefield.

It's almost like the challenge of becoming is really the supreme challenge in life, and one I want to pursue. As artist Erik Pevernagie says: "By 'becoming,' we challenge the range of possibilities in our life." I would add to this that we give ourselves permission to delve inside and consider our own desires, longings, and dreams. It is in these sacred areas that the seeds of identity and destiny are found. They provide a set of clues with which to steer our lives. They awaken avenues that take us beyond prescribed roles and into fulfillment of deepest possibility. This work of becoming taps into the depth of our potential—it allows us to face fear head on and transform it.

Writer Holly Black describes this challenge well: "We all wind up drawn to what we're afraid of, drawn to try to find a way to make ourselves safe from a thing by crawling inside of it, by loving it, by becoming it." Thus, any growth requires tremendous amounts of determination and courage, and a willingness to forge ahead despite uncertainty and doubt.

I somehow managed to avoid this challenge quite readily before firmly committing to pursuing art. It was so much easier to find any other job to do except for the work of becoming an artist. In fact, I almost quit trying to become one before I'd even really given it a shot. There were many times I doubted my passion for art and felt like picking a more clearly defined career would have been so much more straightforward. Embracing the uncertainty of a creative trajectory was difficult for me. And it also meant letting go of garnering approval from those around me. But I also knew deep down inside that I was meant to be an artist through and through, and that to ignore it would be to ignore the reality of my DNA.

There are countless reasons we tend to avoid becoming who we are meant to be in life. I think initially we might be drawn to ideas of what and who we could be because they speak to the reality of a higher life purpose and calling. But we easily devalue our own transformation, for many reasons. First, the evolution calling to us may not be commercially viable, and so, because it can't easily support us, we ignore it. We deem it impractical. We fall into the trap of relegating value (and the scope of what is possible) entirely to the financial realm and miss out on deeper potential inside of us that doesn't readily fit this spectrum.

Second, as mentioned previously, our journeys usually require us to pass several hurdles of fear that are well entrenched in our inner psyches. Many people simply don't want to do the inner work required to jump over these hurdles. Looking inside at limiting beliefs we hold about ourselves and about life can be painful. So by seeking to avoid discomfort, we often cut ourselves and our potential short.

And third, we can easily operate under the delusion that the pursuit beckoning to us requires copious amounts of time that we just don't have. However, all of life's goals, becoming or otherwise, can always be achieved in small steps. In fact, that is the only way anything is achieved at all. Consistent chipping away at something will always result in forward movement towards a greater calling. Even if it's just ten minutes a day, the discipline of doing the work moves us from here to there.

The truth is, nothing can stop you from evolving into who you are meant to be. As the old adage says, we are our own worst enemies. Becoming is simply an intention of the spirit, like every other life choice. It is especially important for Westerners to be reminded that you don't *think* your way into an expanded self, you *live* your way into growth. Our initial intention is simply what sets this expansion in motion energetically. Tiny steps thereafter add fuel to the movement and result in a clearer sense of change over time.

Often the unfolding of the identities we aspire to takes far longer than we prefer, and if we're in a hurry, we may unknowingly sabotage the very progress that we are making. I was thinking about this the other day, how my natural tendency is to assume that once I have a new insight or intention to live out, things will start to be different immediately, of course. But instead, I find the awareness of and desire for a new direction merely positions you to begin a journey with plenty of bumps and jolts, along which you live your way into a new calling.

There isn't a handy road map for this kind of work. It is often a trial and error process, complete with false starts, seeming dead-ends, and plenty of backward and forward movement. The process of becoming is always imperfect and is never as straightforward as one would prefer. This is because all growth really is incremental. I need to be reminded of this often. And we need the reminder collectively, because we live in a society that tells us the exact opposite at almost every turn. The more sellable and exciting line is, *Let's conquer this, arrive at that, achieve this, etc.*—and do it all overnight! Or at least by next week.

Any amount of life experience, though, tells us the exact opposite is more often true. Any growth, in any realm of life, does not happen overnight. You do not just magically arrive at "the next big thing." Growth always happens in small steps and is frankly not that exciting on a daily basis. Much of it can go unnoticed for long periods. But the good news is, over time, one can look back and see, *oh...THAT is how far I've come!* And it can actually be quite far. Real change has happened. But it is not nearly as thrilling as the often false promises society feeds us of immediacy and greatness in one big step. The tale of the tortoise and the hare does have some truth, after all. Although slow and steady may not always "win" the race, it is by far a more accurate description of progress.

So if creativity is a dream planted within you and you sense that it is in some way part of your own journey, be encouraged! Believe in the value of what you are called to. Embrace a long-term approach. Allow change to be a non-rushed process. I remind myself regularly to take a macroscopic view of life instead of a microscopic one. When frustration ensues from staring at the up-close, day-to-day minutia of life and not seeing the strides that we anticipate, it is quite helpful to take a step back (or several) and see the overall arc of life. The movement and growth are much easier to spot. Taking a larger-picture view of life can help us more easily trust that the next step in front of us will indeed play out, just like all the others that came before it. It is ok for maturation to take time. Who you were before is still valid, as is the new thing you are becoming. It is a more truthful picture of reality, and coincidentally a more peaceful experience, to walk hand in hand both with what is and with what someday will be.

Doing this requires becoming adept at letting others' opinions fall by the wayside and instead, listening to an inner voice that is a true compass for your soul's evolution. We all have this voice. It is learning to listen to it that is the challenge. Our own becoming ultimately requires both courage and surrender to this higher knowing. If we refuse to give up and stay on the path, even when that path is less than clear, we will eventually reap the rewards of expanded potential, a more fulfilled life, and a fruitful offering to the world.

— TWO —

The Value of Art in Society

I wasn't raised as an art world consumer. My parents weren't into art, in the official art world sense at least. So while my own creativity was unfettered and free to roam in whatever direction it fancied during my youth, I didn't grow up with exposure to more academic philosophies about art and its importance. My favorite creative memories from childhood aren't of art museums, but of creating dioramas and clay sculptures and other fascinating things on a big table in our garage reserved especially for art making. I came to understand the value of art through an organic process which arose from an everyday person point of view, and not from an art history perspective.

This is important to mention because ironically, I think it forged in me a more expanded view of art and its significance. My exposure to the creative world wasn't attached to a hierarchy. It caused me to clue in to creativity in remote, random corners of the world and not just the official, sanctioned ones. Part of this continued appreciation as an adult has come about as a direct result of living in a neighborhood in LA that is full of artists, musicians, and every possible kind of creative person. Seeing creativity on display everywhere I go has shaped my worldview in significant ways. It has reinforced my democratic view of the arts and a belief in the worthiness of any kind of expression.

One innocent way this began to happen was through my daily walks. Because my neighborhood is full of creatives, there is always something visually interesting going on. People's houses and yards are often very quirky. One neighbor has set some stuffed geese on her shrubs as "yard decor" and they change outfits according to the holiday (right now they are dressed in Easter bonnets). They exude a playful air that makes me smile every time I walk by them. Another neighbor has moved his entire studio outside into his front yard. Every time I pass by, I see paintings on easels in various states of progression and art supplies strewn about. The other month I met a couple who have covered their entire home, inside and out, with mosaic tiles. They have been giving tours of it for years, sharing their creativity with the public.

Chalk drawings on the sidewalks are numerous (and ones by adults too, not just children). I always pay attention to where my feet are going because I never know when I might literally walk over something fascinating. In recent years murals have begun cropping up in unexpected places. And the people who live in the house on the corner just painted one of their trees a bright blue. The entire thing. I love this. I mean, who does something like that?

Artists do. Grassroots creative expressions like these bring tremendous value to my life and speak to me just as much, and often more so, than the ones in galleries. I think this is partly because they often come as unexpected surprises. They feel a bit more pure and unassuming—like they really are just expressions for expression's sake.

But regardless of location or whether the art is sanctioned by someone official or not, creative expression in all forms is a huge bedrock of society. Creativity and the arts have an indelible impact on our lives, whether something serious in a formal setting or something facetious on a street corner. Living in a region of the country where creativity is highly valued has played a huge role in shaping my development as an artist and my view of art. My daily walks show me time and time again that any expression is worth making, none is too small or without significance.

One of the first things I learned about creativity after moving to LA is that, first and foremost, the value of art is intrinsic. People make art because they can't not make art. It is who they are. Just like a scientist will always have a scientific curiosity about life and a mathematician will see the world through numbers, artists, by default, will create. So really, although larger conversations about supporting the arts or where the arts should rank within a humanmade system of value have importance, the deeper issue is that creativity lies in the DNA of artists, and because of *that*, it is inherently valuable. The value is not ascribed from without, it comes from within. Too many artists try to get their art validated externally, from a system that may or may not understand or appreciate what they do. They give more weight to recognition designated by external markers than to their own deep inner belief in their craft. By doing so, they miss the fundamental truth that what they do is of immeasurable value simply because it originates out of who they are.

Art is valuable because it is part of humanity. It is part of how we are wired. Humans have had the impulse to express things since the beginning of time, starting with cavemen drawing on their walls. And so the value of art is innate because it is an integral part of who we are.

If worth is truly inherent and not external, then this reality has the power to flip the commercial gallery world on its head. Creativity of a much broader range, from all corners of the earth, could be celebrated as the powerful expression that it is. When it comes to valuing art, the spotlight that galleries provide can be problematic. Too often what is in the spotlight is declared to be more valuable than what is not, simply because it is seen and meets the specific requirements for being seen (whether that means being large-scale, having commercial appeal, being named worthy by someone of high status, etc.).

But I would say while these are perhaps measures used for showcasing art, they are false measures of worth. To overemphasize the external measures of art can cause us to miss the fundamental reality that art has an intrinsic worth that is entirely its own. If artists truly believed this, their valuing of their work would remain consistent throughout the highs and lows of their careers. They wouldn't be as invested in how many pieces they had sold, whether their work was accepted into a particular show, or if a critique of new work was favorable or not. These kinds of external markers can play a helpful role from time to time, but they do not determine the innate worth of a piece of art. The worth of any creative expression is inherent in the spirit that birthed it. I think this truth alone can bring much freedom and permission to artists to not limit their expressions and to roam outside the box if they desire.

Art and its ability to bring beauty to the world is another reason that its value cannot be overlooked. Art and beauty are intrinsically tied together. Beauty through art elevates us. It inspires us. It offers a different lens through which to see the world. Of course, not all art is a conduit of beauty nor destined to play that role. But for me, creating beauty is a deep passion that fuels much of what I make.

As a child, I grew up surrounded by beauty. My mother put a lot of thought into creating beautiful spaces inside our home and spent time gardening and designing beautiful outdoor spaces in our backyard. Beauty in our environment was a value. And beauty brings much value to our world. Writer Lin Yu-Tang says, "The proper use of imagination is to give beauty to the world...the gift of imagination is used to cast over the commonplace workaday world a veil of beauty and make it throb with our aesthetic enjoyment."

Beauty through art has a unique ability to touch people's lives. It gets us outside of ourselves and takes us to a higher place. It can change our perceptions of the world around us and of others. It has the capacity to reach into deep places within our hearts.

I can speak to this uplifting psychological impact quite readily from my past work in the nonprofit world. I have seen art impact and shape young children's lives in afterschool programs. I have seen the encouraging impact art can have on the homeless time and time again. I've seen how powerful art can be in the lives of women coming out of domestic violence, as both a healing tool and an empowering practice. This is one of the reasons I am such a fan of public art. Although I describe the impact of public art more fully in a later chapter, it should be mentioned here that it is a prime example of art bringing beauty to the world and uplifting neighborhoods as a result. The numerous encounters I had with homeless people during my first mural painting project demonstrated time and time again that the public expression of art was edifying their lives.

Early on during the painting, one man in particular came up to me to talk, and in the course of referencing murals throughout Santa Monica, he said, "And now we have this one!" His use of the word "we" really struck me and made me feel pleased that the homeless community felt a sense of ownership of the public murals—that they truly were "theirs" in some respect.

When I was close to finishing the project I saw him again and joked with him that I hoped someone didn't come tag the mural once it was completed. He looked at me and said, "Oh no, that won't happen! We watch this wall all the time and anyone getting too close, we shoo them away. And you know that mural down on Ocean Park Avenue? Well, that one has a guard." I asked, "A guard?" He replied, "Someone sleeps in front of that mural every night to make sure no one comes up and graffitis it."

This touched me deeply and made me realize anew that art is fundamentally valuable because it touches all of humanity. Great art can liberate both the viewer and the artist alike. This is the gift of the arts for so many people. They provide a mechanism through which things can be expressed that can be expressed no other way. They provide a way for the world to see and hear truths that it would not be able to receive otherwise. It is a gift for both the giver and the receiver. And the value of that cannot really be measured. It transcends the limits of money or status or other more defined measures used to prescribe value. In this way, it is very clear that we must honor and value deeply what is within us as artists, both for our own sake and for the sake of others. The value of what we do should never be called into question. We must assume it and live it without hesitation.

—THREE—
Creative Work and Its Distinctiveness

Creative work is full of paradoxes, something I knew nothing about before embracing an artist's life. It is its own unique beast. It can have a formula and yet at the same time have none. It does not easily fit logical, linear ways of thinking, but sometimes, that is exactly what is needed. There are tried and true principles that can help guide you along the way, but yet there is no overarching road map. It is not a system of working you can really be taught ahead of time; instead, you only learn by diving in. It is work meant for the explorer, not for those who want to see with certainty. It is for the curious and the courageous, and for those in whom the unknown sparks excitement rather than anxiety. It requires being at peace with process and possessing great quantities of internal motivation. It is the epitome of a never-ending puzzle.

The whole cycle of creativity was new to me when I began, and it took me quite a bit of time to figure out the nature of it and understand the distinct rhythms inherent in its execution. I didn't come from a background that taught me any of this, and when I first began my career as an artist, I didn't know any other artists to talk to or learn from. So, learning to work in a new manner involved a pretty steep learning curve for me and lots of trial and error along the way. Figuring it out as I went along became my mode of operating.

Over time, it became pretty apparent why the standard 9 to 5 model does not readily fit the creative process. Creative work has its own recognizable cycles and rhythms, and they don't always line up neatly with the prepackaged categories of mainstream work. To begin with, creativity is a lot more about taking a side road than about taking the highway. It is more about experimentation and not knowing than it is a clearly defined, sequential process. It is about connecting the dots and seeing relationships you didn't see before, arriving at a-ha's in a roundabout way. Creative work is also about being in the flow and not pushing it. It's about learning how to tap in to what is already streaming through you and go with that, not conjuring up something that isn't asking to be birthed and proceeding with brute force.

In creating, unlike in some other kinds of tasks, you're partnering with something beyond yourself. That is why the flow element comes into play. You're joining forces with something that is already moving and wanting to come out. This in and of itself makes creative work different from other kinds of work routines, something I really had no clue about when I started. Many times over the course of my creative career, I've had to return to my personal mantra of "don't push the river." This serves as a reminder to me to take off my boxing gloves and look instead for where the river is flowing and go there. My creative spirit is much happier and more joyful when I do, and inevitably the work I make is more inspired.

The creative process has innate rhythms that require a unique kind of energy. It is a very concentrated energy, similar to the intensity in a laser beam. The kind of intensity required can be sharp and powerful, but it cannot operate continuously. It's like it must be focused, then recharged, focused, recharged, etc., whereas a 9 to 5 model of work is more sustained and constant in energy expenditure. Although it can also include times of intense energy output, it is more often mixed with periods that are rather humdrum—there is an overall day-to-day grind that looks and feels different. The peaks and valleys of energy output are not as high and low, and so they are more sustainable in a day-to-day structure that is more or less the same, week after week.

With creative work, the peaks and valleys are much more apparent, and a varied work structure that allows for this reality is much more effective. When applying focus to a creative project, there isn't really an option to do it half-heartedly or in a semi-checked out state. You either really engage or you don't. There isn't as much of that tedious middle ground, of going through the motions without investing too much. Creative work requires all of you. It is not as easily compartmentalized and is not relegated solely to the intellect. It is a whole body experience involving the mind, emotions, and soul.

Early on, I found it easy to just zero my focus in on the energetic spark that drove the artistic output. And I had no idea what to do when that shut off. It was confusing at times because I didn't understand the ups and downs of the entire cycle. Most importantly, I didn't understand the work that happened during the seemingly "off" times. It was like a whole new animal to learn and figure out.

Slowly I began to focus on learning how to manage the creative cycle effectively, instead of being overtaken by the flow of creative ideas and subsequent excitement or conversely, letting less inspired times keep me from engaging with the process. I discovered that at its core, creative work is really about energy and learning how to channel it and navigate the inherent ups and downs. I also discovered that the intensity of feeling that drove the peaks of the process was not just something to manage, but was also a huge gift, for it was what powered the creativity. In a field with intermittent reward, that is especially needed. It is what helps to sustain the creative path over the long haul. It is a lifeline to bringing forth what is in the depths. Without it, what you make just ends up feeling blah. Channeled intensity is what is needed to create great works of art. It is what makes a stirring piece of music or a thought-provoking piece of writing. Learning to channel this tool of intensity towards the desired artistic outcome becomes key.

Although the energy expenditure and cycle of creativity had a completely different feel from other kinds of work, the discipline and dailyness of it was similar. Diligence was still the name of the game. But, discovering that work could be happening both when measurable progress was being made and also when nothing visible was occurring was new to me.

Creating anything is quite similar to giving birth. A large part of creativity is taking in new stimuli and letting ideas germinate in your being, and then paying attention to when new concepts are ready to emerge. I found that sometimes new works of art wanted to pour out immediately, and other times, they slowly incubated over time and came to fruition years after the seed of the idea was first planted. A distinct period always preceded each creation, whether short or long, from the initial planting of the seed, to it growing in size and finally being executed and brought into the world.

I learned that space in your soul was needed to hold creations before they reached their full mature state. Returning time and again to the birthing analogy became really helpful, as it allowed me to let projects incubate and come out when they were ready. It didn't take too long to learn that forcing projects before their time didn't work. Learning to get in sync with each project's own particular time schedule was really key to producing successful and authentic work. It became very apparent to me that creative work was equal parts internal and external, and learning to honor what was happening in both these worlds was necessary.

Perhaps one of the qualities that most clearly distinguishes creative work from other pursuits is that it often happens with little external reward or prompting. The work is born and driven from a deeper place. Years ago I wrote a blog post about this topic, and a reader's response really brought a lot of clarity to the point I was making. She stated that in many ways, the life of the artist throughout history hasn't changed all that much. A very few are able to enjoy the "fruits" of their labor, meaning a paycheck, an accolade, or even co-workers. She went on to note how compelling the act of creation must be, then, for artists to still create despite this lack of typical reinforcements. This is evidence of a distinctly different energy source than the one that fuels most standard jobs in which the majority of tasks, even if originating from an internal spark of ingenuity, are linked directly to something external (a boss, coworkers, company goals, a deadline, etc.).

As a result, because creative work is so internally driven, you're never really "off." At least not mentally. You don't really leave work in the same way at the end of the day. It is an impulse that can be activated by anything and anywhere. Ideas can come flooding in when you least expect them (and most frequently, it seems, when you are not consciously looking for them). You don't ever shut off your mind from the creative process. It is always operating on some level, even when in the background. I suppose this is true of most self-driven work that requires you to continually create your next opportunity. Creative work necessitates birthing something from nothing, over and over again. It is the epitome of writing your own script.

The ability to both recognize and sustain the internal life force that drives art forward makes creativity both unique and a challenge. And ultimately, it is this internal motivation that moves it beyond the category of work and into the realm of calling. Perhaps that is the best way to really understand the true nature of artistic work. Most artists do the work of creating because they realize they are called to. It is not so much a choice as it is a recognition that the act of creation is a requirement for them, just like food or exercise or rest. Engaging in the work serves as an affirmation to both the artist and the audience of this internal reality.

—FOUR—

Allowing Your Truest Self to Come Forth

Authenticity is appealing. You know it when you see it. There is something innately attractive about someone who is real, open, and transparent. I think the arts allow us to see this side of people more easily than we would otherwise in day to day life. The whole idea behind creating is to express an authentic part of your soul.

One of the best gifts that artists bring to the world through their creations is an honest look at what it is to be human. Artists use their natural ability to fully feel life in all of its nuances and find a way to channel this into expressions that move people.

However, authenticity is not always a guarantee in creative fields. I live in LA, which for some, could be described as the land of inauthenticity. Creative people from all over the world flock here, but many are much more consumed with gaining fame or popularity than they are with honing a genuine creative voice.

Years ago I remember watching a season of *American Idol* and hearing the judges talk about how important it was for the contestants to connect to what they were singing, because when you are able to connect to what you sing, people feel it. And when you don't, the performance tends to fall flat.

I think this can be true of any art form. Another way to describe connecting to what you express is being authentic—the idea that what you're expressing is really coming from an inner place in your soul as opposed to just stemming from a facade. Because a facade, even a well-executed one, doesn't tend to have the emotional impact that a deeper, truer expression does. It lacks a sense of integrity and purity.

One of my favorite contestants on that season was a woman named Siobhan. She struck me as having a true artist's soul. Every time the judges criticized her, she responded with clear reasons as to why she chose the song she did and her thoughts and feelings about it. She was definitely not trying to fit a formula or be who they wanted her to be. She had this inner compulsion to march to the beat of her own drummer, even if it didn't fit a typical Hollywood commercialized category.

Discovering this true, authentic self can take time though, and like all journeys, isn't always clear cut. My own process of discovering my voice was very much a process of trial and error. One of the unexpected benefits of not going to art school was that I wasn't carrying around any preconceived ideas about various art mediums, or well-known artists whose work I should be admiring, or rules around creating in a certain way. So in that sense, I began my art career from a tremendous place of freedom. This served me well because I wasn't operating under any fear of doing something "wrong." All I saw was possibility.

An atmosphere of freedom and possibility is really a powerful nurturer of beginnings because it generates confidence. It allows us to find our own voice and learn to love it. It also helps to stem natural insecurities that pop up along the way as you gain exposure to other artists' work and inevitably compare yourself to them. It's natural to start to wonder from time to time if you should channel your work in the direction of what someone else is doing. Sometimes this pull to go in a different direction can stem from self-doubt, and other times it comes from simple admiration of other artists' work and subsequent inspiration. But, comparison can get in the way of just being who you are. At the end of the day, you are not here to be someone else's voice, you are here to express your own. That is the fundamental basis of art.

Part of finding and expressing my authentic voice over the past several years has involved both tapping into enjoyment and also allowing for change. Joy is a most helpful compass on the creative journey, both for initially finding your voice and for recovering it along the way if it gets lost. It seems to me that the roots of creativity in its purest form are always grounded in joy. It is what makes our souls come alive.

Watching children create is a perfect illustration of this. They are some of the most enthusiastic, authentic creators on the planet. By the time we reach adulthood, too often various mental restrictions creep into our thinking and start to obstruct a creative path that has its own mind about where to go. We need reminders to pay attention to enjoyment because it will always lead us to the next stop on our journey.

One way to do this is to pay attention to what comes

most easily. Often we overlook what is easy and think we must find the hardest way possible. But the reality is, places where we experience ease and flow are signs of gifting and a marker for the way forward. For those of us prone to "shoulds," we may discount this indicator, not seeing it as a reliable direction sign, and instead go a different way that is less life-giving and less reflective of our true nature. We let external influences dominate our own internal sense of knowing. In the process, we live out someone else's expectation of what our voice should be. It behooves us as artists to pay attention to the stirrings in our hearts. They are most likely leading us to a place of fulfillment that is most fitting with our own unique wiring.

Noting places of enjoyment is also a great aid when you're stuck, or in transition, or when a new direction is called for. As I've reminded myself to pay attention to and pursue joy over the years, I've repeatedly found that opportunities will open up in those places, especially if you remain adaptable and open to change. They have not always been the opportunities I was expecting (or even knew to expect), but nevertheless, they always served to expand my art practice and connect me to new people and projects.

Although I began my art career making small collages, a medium I fell in love with early on, I didn't discover my love for building things until I took the plunge and moved into my first studio space in a large warehouse. This was a stretch for me, in the sense that it required leaving the comfort zone of creating in the privacy of my studio at home, but, not only did I finally have a space large enough to build in for the first time, I was also surrounded by other builders...metal workers, furniture makers, a wood shop, and so forth. It was there that I followed the spark to really delve into building large wall sculptures, which led to creating on a bigger scale. This eventually fed directly into my pursuit of mural painting and other large-scale public art opportunities.

But the thing is, I had to allow for each of these transitions to occur. They wouldn't have occurred if I'd shut down the initial spark of interest that fueled their growth. An artistic journey contains many shifts, and part of allowing yourself to grow creatively and stay in touch with the evolution of your authentic self means paying attention to what shifts are happening and allowing for change to occur.

Sometimes when we write or paint or create a film or compose music, etc., we can get too fixated on who we imagine the audience to be, to the detriment of our creative voice. I spent a lot of time early in my art career creating for others, at least in my internal mindset. This didn't have as much of an impact on the actual things I made, per se, but had much more of an influence on my decisions around how and where and to whom I exhibited my art. I very much wanted my art to be a positive influence in the world and to impact others in an uplifting way, so I had a tendency to turn everything I did into what I was giving to other people through my work. For me, this was less about satisfying a demand of the market (as it is for some artists) and more about a genuine desire to make a legitimate difference in the world through my art.

But, whether driven by market forces, a desire to shift culture, or something else, when the idea of impacting other people is given excessive weight and their needs come flooding to the forefront, it is quite easy to lose sight of who you are. Even though I genuinely desired to have my art impact others, I found that creating from this place was not the right place to begin. It tended to be much too heavy and burdensome. I needed to learn to create for myself first.

This was not always easy, as I'd been conditioned in various ways in my past life to be much more aware of others than I was of myself. However, the full spectrum of creativity is bound to be much more free-flowing (and ironically, more powerful) when you listen to what wants to bubble up and let that be expressed before thinking about how you can somehow use what you've made to impact others. It's kind of like putting the cart before the horse. We can too easily lose the organic expression that wants to come forth if we are too focused on external needs.

I found that I tended towards burnout in the few years that I placed the world's interests on top of my art. I slowly came to the realization that if what I made impacted others, great, but it must not drive the initial spark or process. I create simply because it is an essential part of who I am. It is hardwired within me. And the freedom I experience in just allowing the creative impulses that are inside to flow out unfettered ultimately does reach other people. But it is light and free, not heavy or cumbersome. As Howard Thurman is oft-quoted as saying, "Don't ask what the world needs. Ask what makes you come alive, and go do it. Because what the world needs is people who have come alive." We create our most authentic work when we let our art originate from this place of internal aliveness.

A perhaps less obvious marker along the road to discovering our truest creative selves, but one worth mentioning, is limitations of various kinds. Contrary to the tendency to see limitations in any form as something to fight against or resist, the reality is these very limitations can actually serve to guide us in the right direction, much in the same way that enjoyment helps us tap into our voice and gives us clues as to where we need to go next. Whether the constraints we experience come in the form of limited time or finances, restricted space in which to create, physical impediments, or something else, they too can be an aid in discovering our voice if we can learn to see them in this way.

I want to speak to physical limitations in particular, as they especially can be viewed as restrictive rather than as a potentially helpful guide. One of the jobs I had prior to becoming an artist was a well-paid administrative position that was entirely computer based. I had to leave this job solely because of carpal tunnel syndrome and was not able to resume more work like it down the road because of ongoing weakness in my wrists. For a few years, I was even forced to use a mouse controlled by your feet instead of your hands for even short spurts of computer use!

This was disheartening on many levels, not the least of which was the fact that I initially had a lot of resistance to the idea of beginning an art career, thinking instead that I really should be doing a "normal" job, as art didn't count. I felt an urgency to be doing any job except that of an artist. Over time, however, it became clear that this particular physical limitation had been a direct nudge from the universe to begin overcoming the excuses I had used to keep my creativity locked up inside. In some ways, the carpal tunnel forced me to get in touch with what I was really meant to be doing on the planet and to take action toward this. It ultimately became a guide in leading me to a more authentically expressed self.

Physical limitations have also at times guided my own creative process, including the kinds of things I make and the rhythm I follow to create them. One example of this is my vision. I am legally blind in my left eye and it is not correctable, so I use my right eye for everything that is detail oriented. I've often wondered how this affects the appearance of what I make and how my art might look differently if I saw fully with both eyes.

One day in particular, I remember doing a lot of fine detail drawing and really having fun with it. I was in the flow and experiencing a lot of momentum, but soon my eye began to lose its ability to focus (the result of using primarily one eye for many tasks is it tends to wear out quickly). I really wanted to keep going and use the momentum that was building to finish the piece, but I was forced to stop so that my eye could rest. Initially I railed against this need and found it quite frustrating. But over time, I began to surrender to the idea that perhaps the pace at which my eyes allowed me to create was the pace at which I was meant to go. A benefit of going at a slower pace was that it allowed me to access and create from deeper places within my being. It gave me space to search the depths of my most authentic self and bring those things to the surface for expression.

Over the years I have come to learn that so much of my truest self is really meant to create in this way, accessing places that take time to reach. It is what I enjoy and what I crave and where I seem to be most gifted. In a way, being forced to work more slowly than I might have preferred supported the development of this voice that wanted to originate from a place of greater stillness and depth.

I think the most hopeful view of our lives recognizes that all of who we are, including the challenges life throws our way, serves to round out the full picture of who and what we are meant to bring to the world. It all provides clues that aid us in living from a place of inner authenticity. Both the limitations we face and the places of ease and flow we encounter have the ability to become stepping stones that help define the nature of our voice and highlight its distinctiveness. They become marks of our uniqueness.

—FIVE—

Freedom and Keeping an Open Mind

Regularly encountering other artists is very good for me. I think this is in part because it reminds me that anything is possible in the art world. Anything you imagine can be created, any material can be transformed into something inventive, and there are as many ways to approach an art career as there are artists.

Many of us begin creating with very little sense of limitation. There aren't any barriers, our imaginations are free to roam where they wish, and there isn't any agenda other than thinking up something that hasn't existed before. It is ironic, then, that as time goes by, many artists seem to end up being pigeonholed (or pigeonholing themselves) into creating the same piece of art over and over again. While this lends itself well to commerce and a recognizable brand, it doesn't lend itself well to creative freedom.

Early on, I struggled with whether or not I could explore a multitude of visual expressions as I forged a career as an artist, as the official sanctioned path seemed to emphasize a one-track mindset. The preferred formula was to pick one expression or style and not veer from it. And most artists I observed around me seemed to be following along with this. But beyond just feeling constraints from the art world, I also found that to maintain a degree of openness in my creative thinking required a lot of courage. Fear had to be faced and conquered repeatedly in order to keep evolving.

Although this definitely applies to a creative path, this truth can really apply to any area of life. As anyone who has gained some level of proficiency with a skill set knows, learning new things feels like starting over again to some degree. Establishing yourself on a new path, when an old path that took much time and effort to establish already exists, can feel daunting. Even if there is a level of confidence that a new direction will be developed in due time, it can still feel a bit nerve wracking. It's like starting as a newborn again. Sometimes it is easier to think, "Well, maybe I should just stay on the old path. I know it well and I can keep improving there. It's familiar and known." But, it may also be luring you with its sense of safety. And safety isn't always a good thing, especially if it causes you to miss out on growth or a new pursuit that is calling. After all, experiencing creative freedom is one of the foundational joys of art.

One of the most vivid examples of creative freedom I have ever encountered is that of two married artists who live near me in Venice. They are both painters and mosaic artists and over the past fifteen years have turned their entire house, inside and out, into a mosaic tile work of art. Their entire living space is an art project in motion, and they are some of the most inspiring artists I have ever met. The back half of their home is a massive art studio, and the only side of their house that is not covered by mosaic tiles is covered with a huge mural.

This couple lives their art in every way possible. I remember the wife sharing with me that she had spent years in the traditional art world, doing gallery exhibits and pursuing a traditional career path in the arts. She told me that she never found much success there, and that it wasn't until she left it behind that her creativity really took off. As an outside observer, it seems to me that at this point in time her entire life, and the life she has carved out jointly with her husband, is a reflection of purely uninhibited creative freedom. They are most definitely an example of anything being possible with art.

Early on in my career, I remember being stimulated by another artist who creates mail art. She takes letters and postcards and crafts them into mini pieces of art, then mails them out to the artists in her network. They in turn create a response and mail it back. This seemed like a really fun way to connect with other artists, and it served as a reminder to me to keep an open mind when creating and to stay engaged with fun modes of expression. To this day, I still check in with this artist on occasion to see what she's currently working on in her studio. She is one of the most inventive artists I know and is always making something new and different. She is very much an expert at experimentation.

Having an open mind generally comes easily when first beginning anything. But the farther along you go, the easier it is to let your creativity be defined by things outside of yourself. I think creative success in any form can sometimes feed a subconscious belief that if you start to veer from your chosen expression, all the progress you've made will go out the window. Any feelings of having "made it" or having reached certain milestones can inadvertently cause you to fear doing anything outside of the box you've created.

It is really helpful, then, to regularly return to your own definition of what "made it" means for yourself. Value for what we do as artists has to be intrinsic, first and foremost. External value can be added later on, but if we start letting our creative compass be dominated by external voices, we easily lose the pure creative freedom with which we began.

Part of keeping an open mind as we create includes a regular surrendering of preconceived ideas. It is actually necessary to let go of preconceived ideas in order to be in the highest creative flow. Otherwise we stay limited by our human understanding. So, in a way, creating is always a process of surrendering to what wants to be birthed and embracing a high degree of internal freedom in order to do so.

That is what is magical about art. It has a way of knowing what it needs to be ahead of time, and then it goes out into the world and does the job that is programmed into its particular DNA. If you are acting as a midwife of that creative expression, you can't know the code ahead of time. You must operate in faith and simply allow the flow to happen—allowing what wants to come forth and not judging it or putting barriers in its way. Surrendering in this way never fails to return us to a place of freedom, because we see time and time again how the end result is not really up to us. It is more something that comes and reveals itself to us when it is ready. As we experience how these finished works of art impact others in ways we never could have anticipated, we become even more liberated to follow the muse into uncharted territories.

I've always been drawn to artists who create in unconventional ways. The more unusual someone's idea, the more interesting I find it. And I need these other artists for the very reason that they are most often masters at embodying creative freedom. I need to be reminded that art has no limits or rules. They inspire me to throw off any subconscious restrictions I've adopted along the way. It seems that if the creative spirit gets squeezed into too small of a space, freedom usually goes out the window.

I notice this frequently at the higher ends of the commercial spectrum where art starts to look the same, the majority of it taking the form of a large rectangle on the wall. If the craft that brings you passion and life happens to fit these parameters, then great. But if you think of the scope of things that can be made in the world and how many of them don't fit that script, you realize that the art world is not especially conducive to creative freedom. I'll talk about that more in the chapter on commerce. For now, I want to encourage those of you who maybe need permission to explore again, or perhaps for the first time. Exploration never fails to ignite ideas and light a flame for our creative juices! Giving ourselves the gift of freedom in our creative practice is one of the best things we can do for it, both to start it initially and to jumpstart it when it gets stalled.

So much of the fear we feel around letting go of familiar constraints is unfounded. Instead, what I've found to be true is that as you risk and take steps towards a new or undefined thing, the universe will always step in to support you. In this way, you are not alone. So we can start to trust our inner impulses with greater confidence. A photographer friend of mine, who is innately gifted at stepping out in faith to follow creative impulse, describes it as learning to partner with synchronicity—it is the moment when she believes something is possible and opens herself up to look for and receive the support that is already there. She has learned to align her thinking with dreaming and let go of the need to know the "how" of a new dream before acting on it.

Learning to surrender our agenda from time to time permits us to receive and engage with new steps on our creative path that we may not have previously considered. As we get in touch with and create from that free space within, we grow more detached from results and really begin to allow our creativity to grow in ways we could have never imagined. Creative freedom is what keeps the path interesting over the long haul. It is what keeps us returning to the creative well inside to see what might be expressed next.

—SIX—

Encouragement

I think all artists need to be reminded at some point that their creative destinies are worth pursuing over the long haul. They need to be reminded that what they do matters, and that it benefits others. All of us need this support along life's journey, but I think encouragement is all the more important in creative pursuits where the direction is not always clear and external reinforcement is infrequent. Perhaps this is why there is an instant feeling of camaraderie among artists of various stripes. There is a shared recognition of both the value of the arts and also the difficulty of the pursuit.

Encouragement is powerful. Even a single word or interaction can have huge positive consequences. The energy from these moments can result in all sorts of forward momentum and growth. A word of encouragement can be like a cold drink on a hot day, providing the refreshment artists need to keep their creative flow in motion.

There are so many times a fellow artist's words have stirred life in my own creative soul and propelled me forward to new levels. I remember Ken, the manager of the complex that housed my former studio, stopping in my workspace one day to see what I was in the midst of creating. He took some time to look at one of my art pieces, which was growing incrementally on one of my walls. Even in its unfinished state, he saw potential in it and in what it could be and told me I should apply to a public art program for temporary installations at Los Angeles International Airport.

It would never have occurred to me to do this without his suggestion, and in fact, I didn't even know the program existed. I remember feeling a bit intimidated as I researched the application process, as it was quite extensive. Part of me wondered if I was really qualified to be applying, but his words of encouragement and belief in my potential spurred me on to overcome these doubts. I was eventually accepted into their program and as of the writing of this book, am currently on the schedule to build something for the airport this coming year. None of this would have happened without Ken's interest in and encouragement of my work.

Heather is another artist friend who works with a local nonprofit mural organization. It is because of her initiative and belief in my potential that I was able to paint my first ever mural. Her faith in me helped me overcome my fear and do something I'd never done before. Melanie, the manager of Keystone Art Space, encouraged me to rent my first studio, which led to greater community with other artists and much expansion in my art practice. Another friend, Diana, found and offered me my first commission opportunity through her business of connecting artists with collectors. She then coached and encouraged me throughout that process as I learned how to really trust my creative gut in creating a piece of work for a client.

The list could literally go on and on, as there are countless other friends and family who have seen potential in what I am doing and have called it out of me. Each word of encouragement has been a huge force in propelling me forward in a field that is not easy to navigate and sustain. To borrow from author Julia Cameron's vocabulary, I call these people "believing mirrors." There is no artist who does not need these kinds of people along his or her path. Having someone in your life who can affirm your potential is so vital to pursuing any dream.

And the thing is, encouragement is a gift that really does function as a mirror. It is so helpful to have people see things in us that we cannot see. Everyone needs someone to hold a mirror up to them and say, *Look, I see these things in you.* This potential. These gifts. These untapped areas.

We receive it and then are able to mirror it to others, and it becomes a reciprocal entity that actually flourishes best when given away. Because we tend to attract what we give out, in giving encouragement away regularly we are more likely to receive it in return. And so I think one of my jobs as an artist is to give away any encouragement I receive along the way to others, to help them see themselves in a new way. To help support a vision for what they can be, not just what they are. Even a drop of encouragement can cause great expansion in someone else's process. It is like a pebble dropped in a pool of water and its subsequent ripples expand far beyond the initial point of entry. Words of belief and acceptance are like this. They carry a great power.

My artist friend Katherine and I began meeting

regularly several months ago for the sole purpose of being believing mirrors in one another's lives. We were both writing a book and were also both needing extra motivation to keep our respective art practices moving forward. We decided we needed to come together for a meeting of the minds and see what might result.

During one of our coffee chats I shared with Katherine that I'd found a mural painting residency opportunity in Mexico that really excited me. However, I still didn't really consider myself a mural artist. I was a mixed media artist who had happened to paint two murals, but as more of a side project. As I was sharing with her about the opportunity, I also shared my doubts, saying that it seemed the organization had a lot of "real" mural artists already painting for them.

"What do you mean, 'real'?" she asked. "Your murals are real. Do you mean more accomplished?"

And I was like, okay, yes, that is what I mean—artists who have explicitly chosen mural painting as their medium and are well-known for it.

She then went on to encourage me to apply and give it a shot, saying that my murals were as "real" as anyone else's. In effect, she took away my self-doubt as an excuse and in essence pointed out that it wasn't even really valid.

I remember going to an open mic night many years ago. A myriad of different performers got up to sing or play an instrument, or both. Admittedly, as with most open mic nights, while some acts were really good, others were painful to sit through. But what I liked about this particular venue was the support and encouragement given to all. It very much had a "come as you are" vibe. People welcomed one another to the stage, roundly applauded after every performance, good or bad, and generally seemed to enjoy themselves.

I've actually seen this kind of encouragement offered frequently in LA. You might think it would be otherwise, in a metropolis that is overrun with creative types seeking similar opportunities. Instead, I've found that the creative people I've come into contact with are much more likely to offer genuine appreciation and support of one another's efforts than they are to criticize or compete.

This is so important when it comes to creativity. Even though improving one's craft is also important, evaluating any art form based on skill alone only takes you so far. Art's ability to move people is based on many more subjective factors than solely the execution of the outer shell. When you bring understanding and encouragement to the mix, people can express themselves in an environment of acceptance. I think this bodes well for creative flourishing. When we are accepted, fear goes out the window. And without fear, creativity becomes fully unleashed to grow in all kinds of ways. So, encouraging words along the way are not merely a nicety or an insignificant blip on the radar. They truly have the potential to form a solid foundation for sustained creative growth over the long haul.

Not only do we need to offer this acceptance and encouragement to others, we need to offer it to ourselves. This is perhaps one of the best things we can do to support our creative practice. Our ability to grow in creative confidence stems from a groundwork of acceptance. I need to remind myself of this often when my internal critic rears its head and threatens to sabotage my creative process. Artists are often their own worst critics.

But we have a choice as to what voice we will tune in

to. We can make a conscious decision to turn away from the inner critic and instead, tune in to a gentler voice that is encouraging and patient with failure and with incremental growth and progress. After all, we can't force the baby. It must be allowed to come in due time and in its own way. As we accept ourselves and our ability at its current level, we offer ourselves massive support for moving to the next level. Encouragement helps us both recognize and be patient with the small shifts in our progress. It sharpens our perception to notice even slight gains in forward movement. And it ushers in a peaceful, internal state of confidence that flows right into our creative thriving.

— SEVEN —

Being Misunderstood

Early on in my creative journey, a romanticized comment about artists sipping wine and dreamily dabbing a canvas with a paint brush clued me in to the fact that artists are not easily understood by those around them. It made me realize that there are a lot of misconceptions out there about what it means to actually be someone who claims the identity of artist and takes steps to live it out.

I think if people really understood the reality of making art, promoting yourself, and sustaining a creative spark over the long haul, there would be far fewer romanticized notions about it. Some of the misunderstanding around artists comes in part because the pursuit of art doesn't fit nicely with the linear, black and white thinking that we're regularly taught with regards to career. It is much more of an intuitive, non-linear process that is primarily self-driven. It often does not compensate well or give other types of external rewards, which makes it all the more confusing for those on the outside peering in.

It can be difficult for others to fully understand the

exact process or the motivations that drive it. I also find that many people simply don't know how to talk about creativity, even if they are supportive in a general sense. They don't know how to talk about an artist's latest direction, or celebrate getting over a creative block, or recognize that many times creative expression signifies a triumph over inner doubts. As I previously mentioned, I think this is partly because the creative work process is so different from the more logical routine of a typical career. It is not as easily quantifiable, there is an element of the unknown to it, and it is most definitely not a clear, succinct path. Even if well-meaning people sincerely want to know how an artist's career is going, it is not something they always know how to engage with or approach.

Finding community as artists, then, becomes quite essential to help mitigate experiences of being an anomaly. Community with other creative types has been incredibly helpful for me, both to mirror understanding and also provide a sense of camaraderie.

I found an abundance of this kind of camaraderie when I moved to Los Angeles from San Jose. There is an incredible creative energy in LA that I hadn't experienced anywhere else previously. It seemed that almost everyone I met was pursuing a creative dream of some sort. I remember reviewing in my head every person I'd gotten to know in the first few months of living here and being amazed that literally every single one was doing something creative. That had never happened anywhere else I'd ever lived.

Even watching random people in my neighborhood who were clearly creative contributed to this sense of shared calling and community. My next-door neighbors, who I see often from my kitchen window, most definitely have a creative aura about them. I often see the wife spray painting or nailing things together in their courtyard. Her husband dresses in a somewhat old-fashioned, but interesting way, frequently wearing sophisticated hats and suspenders. They habitually carry paint brushes or odd-looking tools and are always in the process of building various contraptions in their driveway. They simply exude a creative air. And, they are in their mid-60s, which inspires me as well. It regularly reminds me that creative work is not something from which you ever retire.

Living in a town that supports people of all ages pursuing art in one form or another has affirmed my own chosen path. Meeting so many like-minded people has contributed greatly to the experience of a larger community that understands the uniqueness and challenges of a creative life.

In contrast to this, I found during my few years of living in Silicon Valley that telling people you were an artist was a surefire way to stop a conversation. In fact, I remember attending a friend's party back in San Jose, a few years after having moved to LA. Almost every single person in the room was employed in the tech industry. As I made small talk and began telling people that I was an artist in response to the "What do you do" question, the conversation literally did stop. Or at least slowed way down. One person said to me, hesitantly, in response, "Is that like sketching on the streets? I saw someone in Paris doing that." No one seemed to know quite how to respond to this career choice, or even ask about it or discuss it.

It was such an odd experience for me, especially coming on the heels of a few years in LA where discussing one's creative pursuits was as commonplace as talking about the weather. Working outside of a corporate structure can be difficult to understand if it hasn't been your experience, and so in that sense, the people at the party were just responding out of what they knew (or didn't know). But this is all the more reason why a community of artists is so crucial. An art career is not the mainstream path, and so support and understanding is vital to living it out.

If a community of artists isn't readily apparent where you live, try seeking it out. I've found that artists almost always seem to say yes to chances to connect with other artists. We support one another's projects, root for one another's successes, and offer encouragement when we're stuck. I've found that artists genuinely want to support and believe in one another. This has been true of every artist group I've joined, every studio complex where I've rented space, every public art endeavor, and every gallery exhibit. Artists are in one another's corner.

And if something tangible doesn't exist where you are, you can create it yourself. A friend of mine who lives in a neighborhood where there aren't as many creative people decided to do something about it and started hosting a monthly drawing night. She initially contacted me and another artist who wanted to support her efforts, and between the three of us, plans are in the works for it to expand and grow. Another woman I know began hosting "art socials" and invited her neighbors to come and learn a new craft each week that she would prepare and teach. Camaraderie truly does wonders to provide a sense of shared understanding and support.

Misunderstanding can also arise from the detractors, or from those who like to cast doubt on the pursuit of dreams. Once you decide to follow a dream and assert your creative voice into the world, these people love to come out of the closet. I think this is why a large part of the creative journey is an inner one. It involves learning how to trust your own voice and getting to the point where you can firmly believe in what you are creating and in the dream you are pursuing, regardless of the naysayers. Possessing this internal belief makes it far easier to keep taking steps towards a calling and to shrug off commentary that isn't constructive. Being misunderstood is a part of life, and although it's especially pronounced in the arts, it's something that is only overcome by having a strong center.

Developing this strong center takes time, especially when we are just starting out. I find it helpful in the early stages of finding and expressing your creative voice to surround yourself with encouraging input, people who can affirm who you are becoming even if you are not there just yet. Later on, once we have developed a stronger sense of our creative expression and are able to put it out into the world more boldly, we can more easily withstand the critics who come our way.

Part of developing this strong internal confidence comes from learning to trust our intuition about how things should be as we create. It takes some practice to learn to identify and trust our gut impulses in the studio, and also an ability to hold our creations freely and allow them to become what they are meant to be. But the more we learn to both trust our growing skills and also listen for guidance as we create (and that guidance always comes, if we really tune in), the more we are able to create from a place of strength and confidence. As our internal core strengthens, we are less dependent on something external to mirror back what we already know to be true.

It is in developing our strong center that we follow our own divine spark. This is where we are most powerful. This is where we find the most fulfillment and where our gifts best intersect with the world's needs. It becomes necessary to give more weight to our internal knowing of who we are and what we are meant to do on this planet than to the wonderings of the culture around us.

We can learn from famous artists or writers in this respect, those who went before us and were perhaps only truly celebrated after their death. Their work was maybe ahead of its time or not fully seen or understood until long after their season on the planet had passed. Many of them were hidden from the powers that be most of their lives and were only really discovered after they were gone. But as beneficiaries of their work today, we can be grateful they didn't give in to whatever doubts they may have faced from those around them. The world would never have been gifted their work otherwise. Their perseverance and commitment to their creative callings impacted the larger culture for the better. In the same way, artists in general, well-known or not, often act as forerunners, their work being a precursor of something to come. It is in this way that they help move culture forward.

And so then, it takes courage to remain true to who you are and the work you are called to do, especially in the face of misunderstanding, criticism, or doubt. However, those things are never a gauge for whether the work you are called to do is worth doing. As artists we need to routinely return to our innate knowing and trust it. We must do this over and over again, both with the actual things we create and with choosing to adhere to a pursuit that may not make sense to those around us. It is as we align with this strong inner core that our true power is released into the world. It is by knowing who we are and firmly committing to living it out that we become the most effective versions of ourselves for the benefit of the culture around us.

—EIGHT—

Creating When You Don't Feel Like It

Today I have dragged myself to Pepperdine University to get some uninterrupted writing time in. Not that Pepperdine is anything to complain about. It is in a prime location on a pristine bluff overlooking the Pacific Ocean—the ultimate college campus, in my mind. On this particular writing day, sequestering myself away somewhere outside of the house was necessary to continue plowing along on my first draft.

Many authors have written about the oh-so-common experience of having to overcome great resistance to one's particular creative pursuit. However, I've most often heard this topic addressed with a "fight through resistance at any cost" approach, something akin to a massive onslaught of sheer will. Sometimes, yes, this is called for. But sometimes it is not. Sometimes a gentler approach is a much more appropriate way to overcome blocks or coax our inner artistry to emerge from hiding.

But first, I must lend my own two cents to the truth of creativity being mostly about diligence and discipline and less about grand inspiration. Every creative person who earnestly pursues his or her craft knows exactly what it is to have to push forward, regardless of whether they feel ready or inspired. This is probably Creativity 101. In this respect, any creative work must be looked at in the exact same way you would look at a job with an actual supervisor. Although the nature of creative work will vary in many other ways, in this instance, it is no different. For any progress to occur, there really isn't an option of not showing up.

Even tiny amounts of persistence keep the wheel greased and facilitate forward movement. And the good news is, forward movement itself is really what's important, more than the exact amount of time you can give on any particular day. I've found that whether I have two hours or twenty minutes for whatever my current project is, just attending to it at all keeps me connected to its creative rhythm. But if I miss those regular connections, I quickly lose touch with the energy that is driving the project—which makes it that much harder to resume.

Creativity is something that needs to be fed, and it gets fed when we show up for it. As we learn to show up for it on a regular basis, it can grow and develop a life of its own. Ideally, this life then feeds us in return, so the process can become like a mutual exchange. We feed it, it feeds us, and we're on the way together.

However, consistently staying the course is anything but easy. As Steven Pressfield so eloquently wrote in *The War of Art*, "The more important a call or action is to our soul's evolution, the more resistance we will feel toward pursuing it." Even in the writing of this book, I felt like I was back at a creative beginning of sorts, not dissimilar to when I first became an artist. I found I had tremendous resistance to the daily act of writing, and although I clearly knew it was the next creative expression that needed to come through me, getting into a regular, disciplined rhythm was extremely hard.

It was helpful to remind myself that I had gone through a similar journey when I first began creating art. And that, over time, this daily rhythm became a more natural part of my being, much in the same way jogging or some other exercise starts to become a part of you after pushing through the initial hard stages of learning a new habit.

Resistance, then, can be battled in part by learning to place a high value on incremental, consistent progress. To do this, it helps tremendously to tune out the culture we live in from time to time, for we live in a culture that only knows how to celebrate big, public successes and finished products (thank you social media). Progress that looks minimal from an outside perspective isn't rewarded. The dailyness of life tends to be eschewed. But unfortunately, the only way to live life *is* daily. The only way to make progress on anything requires consistent, repetitive effort which is far from glamorous moment to moment. We must not undervalue this fundamental reality of movement.

Creativity is activated as you spend small amounts of time on it in habitual intervals. Even spending a few minutes of concentrated energy planning for next steps, envisioning a new project, or sketching an idea "counts." It is like a muscle. With use, it grows. Without use, it atrophies. So don't be discouraged by progress happening in tiny increments, or by the larger culture's frequent discounting of this reality of life. That is the only way progress towards anything worth doing is made. Life is lived one moment to the next. We receive whatever movement comes as a result—and we learn to let that be enough.

As I mentioned at the start, sometimes a more brute force, "make it happen" mentality is needed to show up for our art. Sometimes. But I have also learned that this is not prescriptive for all situations. Sometimes we're stuck or not moving forward because of an emotional block, or because we're physically tired, or because our inner artist is starved for nurture. Sometimes feeding ourselves first is the best way to get back on track creatively. The inner creative well seems to respond quite affably to self-nurture. Sitting awhile in nature can do wonders for our ability to pick up where we left off. Sometimes gentleness with self is what is called for. Our artist selves aren't in the military, after all. So a militaristic approach might garner success the first few times we employ it, but over the long haul it can have a way of backfiring and resulting in burnout. Gentleness can turn out to be quite effective for our artistry. It can be a much better tool for eliciting flow.

I speak from experience on this. I used to be the queen of the "make it happen" mentality. I'd like to say I've become more balanced in my mid-life years. I think I have. But it hasn't come without some growing pains. Learning to be more gentle with myself has certainly been one key. I've found that sometimes creativity needs to be coaxed out. Nudging ourselves in this way is almost akin to tricking ourselves into creating. This is especially important for projects where there is no external boss or client, which is true of many fine art pursuits.

It is amazing how many other things can get done when you're staring a looming project in the face...the house gets cleaned, the trash is taken out, messes are organized. Productivity in pretty much every other area of life seems to skyrocket.

When these situations arise, I find it helpful to woo myself in a variety of ways. Like, ok, I need to write a chapter, how about I go sit on a bench in a shaded park to do it? I'm much more likely to get it done this way than if I stay in the house and hope I'll magically overcome the myriad of distractions there. Or when it comes to art, even convincing myself to just spend ten minutes in the studio is usually an effective trick. Ten minutes can always be agreed to, no matter how fierce one's inner resistance or how demanding one's schedule. And then, ninety-nine percent of the time, the ten minutes easily turns into a much longer period of sustained work.

Consistent creative progress is kind of like exercise. We all want the benefits of it and know it's good for us, but have to constantly remove mental roadblocks to get there. But really, the hardest part is just getting out the door to begin. Mind tricks in the form of gentle, doable suggestions then become quite helpful.

Sometimes gentleness is best employed by showing up regularly for our creative work and then committing to not judge whatever comes forth. A suspension of agenda is called for. The discipline is revealed in our consistency in showing up regardless of feeling or inspiration, but what flows out during the work session isn't really up to us. So we can release the inner judge that so often shuts down the process and learn to gently accept and encourage the work that emerges.

A big part of employing gentleness in this way is letting go of a need to have things figured out prematurely.

Instead, we learn how to let things unfold. We let go of outcome. Holding our art gently frees us from the grip of internal constraints that try to shut down the process. When something is trying to birth itself, the last thing you want to do is restrain it. Yet there are so many ways we do this inadvertently...preconceived ideas, notions of good and bad, external expectations, internal ones, shoulds, should nots, etc.

When I can clear my mind of any such baggage, the art is then free to come out the way it needs to. This is what makes it so interesting to watch, because I am not really sure what's going to happen next or how it will resolve. Even though I'm participating in the creation, there is a part of me that is just an interested observer. At its core, creativity is like one big exercise in learning to be present and responding to exactly what is happening in the current moment. We don't need to get fixated on an overarching plan. The overarching plan can sometimes just get in the way of the here and now and manage to keep us stuck. But it is in the here and now that we're being given the direction we need, as we repeatedly show up and do the work and then stay detached from any results.

Co-creating is a good descriptor of this process—the ability to watch for synchronicity and guidance, either from our own intuition or outside of ourselves, and partner with it. It seems to be the healthier middle ground between a making it happen mentality and passivity. Co-creating allows for both action and listening. I would go so far as to call it the essence of sustainable action. Our inner artist becomes a self that we learn to partner with as we move forward with our goals. Some people call it an intuitive knowing, others call it a life force, but regardless

CREATING WHEN YOU DON'T FEEL LIKE IT

of name, it is something we learn to channel. As we learn to recognize what is unfolding and partner with it, we are led into a more organic process that flows in a much more continuous manner than the more strained pattern of fits and starts that is characteristic of forcing things to happen. We become active listeners to our own creative energies. We become masters at paying attention to the creative undercurrent that is always flowing somewhere inside, and we learn how to respond in ways that best support its direction and flow.

One tool that has helped me either stay with or rediscover creative flow is learning to see my overall creativity as a palette. Someone spoke to me years ago about the connection between the various creative outlets in my life. He used the analogy of a painter's palette, which has a multitude of colors side by side, each available to be mixed with the others. He compared this synergy to bees cross-pollinating as they zip from flower to flower. Engaging in one art form creates flow in another area, and vice versa.

This has been very true for me as I observe the ways music, writing, and art intersect in my life. It's like something gets unblocked in one area when I switch modalities. So whether it is an observation that I sit down and write about, a song I sit down to play, or any other act that fosters creative movement, they all in turn give life to my art-making process.

Even beyond explicitly creative pursuits, a variety of actions can be a way to jumpstart ourselves if we feel resistance towards our daily movement. Take a walk. Bake a cake. Write free form in a journal. See your creative output as larger than just your current area of focus. Engaging in as large a creative flow as possible brings life to areas that might feel stuck or uninspired. One artist I know goes for a long run when she feels blocked. Another collects seashells on the beach. Even driving in the car for stretches of time can be quite helpful. I've often found solutions to my creative problems come to me when I'm in the car, as my brain has time to enter a different space that allows for mulling over various possibilities and solutions.

Taking this "painter's palette" view of my creative life can sometimes be a challenge for me, as I tend to be very focused and goal-oriented. I often find it hard to give myself permission to do these seemingly unrelated other things. But if we're actually operating in a much larger field of creativity than what we see right in front of us, then these "other things" are in fact quite related. They are energetically connected to the project that has our current attention.

When I first encountered resistance to writing this book, I decided to start making daily drawings. The drawing had no agenda, no end goal in mind. There was no finished product I was trying to achieve. Just draw, scribble, color, express. I did this for thirty minutes a day and was surprised at the creative flow that opened up as a result—not just with my writing, but in other unexpected areas as well. It is tremendously helpful to think of creativity as a large container that houses many things, as opposed to just our particular medium or career focus, and of all these things as playing a role in moving us forward towards our creative potential.

If nothing else, our experience of resistance is a clue to the value of the work in front of us. If there was no value to art, it wouldn't require any effort. There would be nothing to overcome. And so on days when I want to do anything but create, I remind myself of the value of what I am called to do. As the axiom says, anything worth doing is worth fighting for.

And it is a fight on many days, believe me. Resistance has all sorts of ways of rearing its head. But fortunately, creativity is like a pilot light. It is always burning, even if the heater it powers isn't running. If we just show up to engage with the canvas or the page or the music score, we can access that pilot light, however weak it may seem. If we engage with it repeatedly, our creativity will fire up eventually. The same creative voice that spoke through us in the past is still there beneath the surface, available to be coaxed out one little bit at a time. True success in the arts could be summed up by a simple refusal to give up. Our part is to just be faithful, to return and try again.

— NINE —

Commerce

Recently a particular art opening caught my eye. A woman I know, who is a phenomenal artist and very active in the LA art scene, was the curator and the show was full of fascinating work.

I decided to go check it out, and in the midst of feeling very inspired after attending, recognized that I hadn't felt this way in a long time after an art opening. As I was thinking about the variety of work that had been on display, I realized that none of it was easily sellable (couldn't be easily moved, was an awkward size or shape, etc.). Much of the work, which was more installation-based, was unlikely to sell at all without a tremendous amount of effort.

I was talking about these observations with my friend afterwards, and telling him that there was a connection between the level of inspiration and the difficulty of selling these particular works, at least in my mind. Sometimes the most awe-inspiring art is the least commercially driven. Or, put another way, what lends itself to good business is not always the best art.

For me personally, creativity has never been about a formula. Creativity may lead to a formula, which is then what can more easily lead to money. But too often I've seen artists start with creativity, end up with a formula, and then never return to creativity again. The formula dictates almost the totality of what they do. This is why commerce and creativity, at best, have a very tenuous relationship, and at worst, end up in a constant state of competition. It is why more commercialized art forms that focus on mass production, finding a successful formula, and speed aren't as appealing to me. I am wired in a way that leads me to create from deep places in my soul, and this isn't always conducive to market appeal.

I first had this realization years ago when I moved to LA. I was working for a couple who produced their own line of greeting cards, and they needed artists to draw the designs for them. The bulk of the job consisted of making hundreds of designs at a time for each card—really, the epitome of mass production. Naturally, the designs would shift to accommodate the holidays and what the market was demanding.

This experience was a really good learning opportunity for me, as it gave me a chance to see what it felt like when my creativity was turned into a mass-produced product. Obviously, this orientation worked well for this couple and their particular goals. But for me, it was rather soul killing. I felt like any creative spark that may have been there initially quickly faded as one repetitive design after another was churned out.

I have found over the years that I am not alone with this feeling. Many artists I know who burn out often do so because they get tired of the commercial side of art—of having to be a robot producing piece after similar piece and not feeling free to let their muse take the reins and lead them in new and unexpected directions.

It is unfortunate that commoditizing things at the expense of creative exploration can end up killing the very creative spirit that leads many to art in the first place. That is why art is such a tricky business (figuratively and literally). On one hand, there are good things about selling art. Art has value in society, and one way our particular society ascribes value is through money. So, selling art in itself is not necessarily a problem. But when money becomes the sole factor in making creative decisions, the wrong things start to get prioritized.

We need to be honest about the effects of commerce on art making, since we live in a society that routinely implies that money is the only value scale (which of course isn't true). This can be problematic for the creative who really wants to be inventive. Strict parameters on what will sell create limitations that impede expression. And defining creative expression too narrowly is often a huge disservice to both the artist and society as a whole.

The farther you go along an artistic career path, the more you start to realize that it is very easy to lose sight of the origins of creativity—the impetus to create for creating's sake. There is something very pure about this form of creating, and the kind of artists who operate from this place make the kind of work that I find most fascinating. There is something about adding commerce to the mix that can so easily dilute this potent creativity (think of a giant Hollywood blockbuster that rakes in money but is basically terrible, special effects replacing plot and substance, versus an excellent independent film that makes hardly anything, but is engaging, thoughtful, and offers something you've never seen before).

Early on in my career, I attended a fellow artist's show at a well-known art gallery in Santa Monica. Afterwards, I realized I had a choice to make. Did I want to go wholeheartedly in the gallery representation direction (which very much emphasizes the business side of art)? If so, I realized that it would significantly impact the kind of art I made. At the time, I wasn't willing to make the trade-off of restricted creative expression for possible greater commercial gain.

The reality is, I often make things that aren't very easy to sell. One of the shifts I've made in my art making over the years is towards building 3-D wall sculptures out of book materials. None of these creations are pieces of art you can easily pick up and hang on a nail. They're actually quite time consuming and tedious to hang, and most people wouldn't bother to go to the trouble. But their complexity is what makes them visually interesting. And I value this far more than saleability or commercialism.

The gift of self-expression is what has primarily motivated me and sustained me over years of art making. When I made a conscious choice to move away from framed (sellable) art for a period to explore creating on walls, I remember feeling a sense of limitlessness. This decision opened up the parameters of what was creatively possible. It was like I could feel my brain expanding even thinking about walls or entire rooms versus being limited to a traditional piece of canvas on a wall. I went through a period of feeling "done" with the rectangle.

The truth is that deep down I feel more integrity when I express what is longing to be expressed than when

I modify it or contain it to get it to either make more money or appeal to more people. And in the process of following these sorts of unbounded creativity cues to expand my art practice, my sense of creative fulfillment has grown exponentially. Purity of expression is what I find most meaningful, and everything else falls somewhere farther down on the hierarchy. I have found art to be most freeing when it is approached more as a means of living life than as a primary means of making a living.

Lest you think otherwise, this chapter isn't so much about criticizing the role of commerce as it is about challenging commonly held cultural beliefs about money that creep into the art world and affect it in a negative way. And it is also about encouraging artists to preserve their creative integrity, because that is the best gift they have to offer the world.

A few years go, I was part of an artist critique group. We took turns visiting each other's studios and giving feedback on one another's work. The discussion around one particular member's paintings stood out to me, as it illustrated this tension between commerce and purity of expression. This artist's paintings were created on some very fragile materials, which in my mind fit very nicely with the sense of impermanence and fragility of the lives of the urban youth who were her subject matter. To accompany the paintings, she had made soundtracks of the youth speaking and sharing about the challenges of living in an urban neighborhood.

Several people offered comments of concern regarding the fragility of her materials, wondering if they were archival and how collectors would feel about it, and how she would be able to exhibit these pieces in gallery settings.

To me, all the suggestions regarding how to fix the impermanent feeling of the materials, although practical, would have resulted in making the work far less interesting and also would have taken away something central to the story the art was trying to tell.

So often, commercial concerns serve to sterilize art instead of truly support creativity. The very strength of a particular work can be so easily diminished for the sake of the market. There are no easy answers for these tensions, but thinking about them critically can at least help inform the direction you want to go.

Sometimes the more money comes into play, the more easily art can become just about success or image and not about creativity. Conversely, having less money can spur all kinds of ingenuity. Awhile back I came across two guys on Twitter who had just started a Web series focusing exclusively on the stories of artists who operated outside of traditional art hubs. At the time I learned about them, their budget was $40 a month, and with that they somehow managed to make fascinating mini documentaries on these artists' lives. The stories they told were quite refreshing, in part because the whole project felt very grassroots and honest and real. As a result, the art they featured felt that much more inspired and free. I think this was partially due to the lack of ties to vast sums of money and the restrictions that come with it. Sometimes we are most creative when we have a limited amount of resources available and are forced to take our inventiveness to a whole new level.

All artists at one point or another have to face a decision about whether or not to create for the market, and to what degree. If creating for the market exclusively aligns with your goals like it did for the card-making couple I worked for, then great. Some people are comfortable with the limited parameters commerce brings to the mix. Others are more motivated by art sales than by self-expression.

But this choice is not without significant impact on one's creativity, and I think awareness of the impact that commercial limits bring to the creative process is key for sustaining an art practice over the long haul. In order to keep expression alive over the long term, it is essential to remember to carve the path you want and not give in to pressure to make your art fit a certain category. Simply put, there are far easier ways to make money. And if we lose the will to create in pursuit of a certain level of financial compensation from our art, then what is the point? What is most important is lost.

With regard to commerce, the most necessary thing is to make a conscious choice about the relationship you want to have with it. Choose the degree to which you want to engage and be careful to preserve your creative integrity along the way. Most important, don't buy into the false belief that in order to be a "serious" artist, you must make a living from your art. This just isn't true. All that commerce really signifies is a set of parameters. That's it. A choice to de-prioritize these parameters in the arts will always puzzle people who don't understand the artist mind. A value for beauty and expression above money befuddles them. However, it makes logical sense that non-commercialism is much more deeply tied to self-expression. The first fosters the second. Unduly pressuring one's work to produce monetary results is a surefire way to take away the experimentation factor, which is so integral to creative growth and fostering potentially powerful expressions. Money is not the only way of measuring worth. Sometimes readily accepted cultural norms like these need to be questioned—and really, who better to do that than artists?

—TEN—

The Ebb and Flow

I live by the ocean, and this is not by accident. Something deep within me responds to water, and one of my favorite ways to spend time is sitting at the water's edge, watching the incoming waves crash against the shore and then slip back out to sea. The rhythm is mesmerizing and calming.

Nature has often been a helpful metaphor that has affirmed over and over again the natural ebb and flow of the creative cycle. Dormancy and activity. Hiddenness and visibility. One thing creativity is not is a machine. It is far too nuanced for that. Of course, it is possible to make it into a machine, and there are people who do. But that process then becomes something quite different. It is no longer Art with a capital A. It may still be something creative or inventive, but a different mechanism for producing has taken over. So when I talk about the cycle of the creative flow, it is with Art in mind that I do so.

The cycle of art can appear quite contradictory, and it took me awhile to figure this out. Previous jobs hadn't prepared me to understand work that is both inner and outer, seen and unseen. Because of this, I didn't initially pay attention to the fact that some of the best creative ideas could come when you are seemingly doing nothing, i.e. in the shower, or taking a walk. I didn't fully understand how connected all parts of life were to the creative cycle. It was very easy to look at inward-focused times as divorced from creativity. The only obvious category for creative work was the outward-focused one. That's why I felt compelled to go from one project to the next and ignore any inner compass directing me to explore, play, or experiment with new ideas.

But the very reason creativity is good for the human soul is because it is both inner and outer—it encompasses the whole person. And it is its nature to ebb and flow. It does not surge out of us as some continuous, unchanging force, like water from a fire hydrant. It is more like a river that meanders, sometimes flowing strongly, other times flowing more quietly, depending on the season.

Fairly early on, I realized that detaching can serve the artist well in navigating this ebb and flow. People who are deep feelers, as many artists are, can easily get overly attached to the variety of emotions that help drive the creative act. Given this tendency, it is extremely helpful to take a step back from both the highs and the lows and look at the entire creative process from more of an observer role. The pursuit of art, after all, is the epitome of holding things loosely. Detachment allows us to ride the up and down waves of the creative life and still function well. It assists in ushering in a state of emotional equilibrium. And it is in the experience of emotional equilibrium that we can find a sense of peace. This allows us to create from a place of internal rest that provides fuel for the entire process.

This is true in the active seasons that are driven by a stronger sense of creative energy, but it is perhaps even more helpful in the quiet seasons, the times when there is no felt energy and nothing tangible to engage with. Sometimes, despite our best efforts at creating regularly, there are longer periods of silence in our creative lives. I call these periods the dormant season. The times where there is nothing visible happening. Those times when it feels like the creative well has shut off completely. These seasons can be much more challenging to navigate. Often, it is the times that are more "ebb" than "flow" that are most difficult to wade through and that require a long look at the larger picture. It is in these times that we need help learning how to nurture and allow for inward periods that can later produce great works of art and music.

During many of the dormant periods I've lived through, my daily walks have frequently provided me with the perspective shifts I've needed to persevere along the way. Nature, it seems, is full of analogies and is an excellent reminder that no one can be in bloom full-time.

I remember taking one such walk during a several-month stretch where my creative well seemed to have shut off entirely. No amount of coaxing of my inner artist seemed to work. When I tried to show up to daily work sessions, nothing emerged. The insides of me, which were usually teeming with creative life, felt empty and dead. There was no creative fire, no discernible spark, nothing. For the first few weeks, this felt rather painful, but I figured it would pass any day. But as this dormant period stretched on to occupy several months, I began to wonder if I'd ever create again. I wondered if I'd ever have another imaginative flicker or if my career had perhaps ended prematurely.

Catastrophic thoughts like this began to pop into my head and fill my mind with their tempting untruths.

On this particular walk, I remember being fascinated by several trees that had enormous root systems visible to the eye—you could see the tops of their roots spreading across the ground in a wide arc and then proceeding to bury themselves deep within the earth. They didn't have any leaves on them at the time, as it was winter (well, as winter as it can be in Los Angeles), but it reminded me that even if a tree isn't blooming, growth is still happening underneath. There is a massive root system still in play.

In a similar way, the creative life needs its own root system to sustain it through the cycle of ups and downs. I've come to believe that our creative lives operate in much the same way as these trees. The root system that supports the entire thing has a chance to expand underground during the dormant times. This growth is hidden from our view, but it is from this root system that exciting inventions and creations later come forth in the more active and visible times.

Months afterward, when I had emerged from this period of creative nothingness, I was sharing with a friend that one day during this bleak period I had been sitting in my studio, unsure of what to do or how to move forward, when the outline for this very book popped into my head. It was the *faintest* of ideas—so faint that I almost didn't perceive it. But I took a chance and just wrote down the tentative title and chapter ideas that seemed to float ever so imperceptibly in the air around me. And then I folded up the notes and put them away and didn't revisit them until much later.

But this proved to me that important things can

emerge and take root in the times where it feels like nothing is happening. Space is needed for new creations to develop and surface. Periods of wandering can allow for exploration and discovery. Sometimes it can feel like we're on "pause" from an external point of view, but it is in the pause times when some of the deepest internal work and change is occurring. The inner soil is quite fertile.

This goes against conventional wisdom (or American cultural norms) that advise us to run from any pause in life, or see it as something to escape prematurely. I think I've learned the opposite over the years. The creative cycle actually needs these periods, and I need to allow for them when they occur. The pause allows us to get back to our true center, to a place of rootedness. It allows for time and space to see the hamster wheel of ceaseless activity for what it is, a spinning wheel with no mooring. In the pause we are given clarity to shift what needs to be shifted so that our future times of active growth are anchored in a clearer sense of direction and purpose. Our roots grow broader and deeper in the winter times so that come summer, our next surge of visible creations can grow in expansiveness and be powered from a stronger base.

We need encouragement to remember that creativity can be just as much an inner, hidden process as it is a visible, outward act. I've come to realize that just as the cycle itself naturally ebbs and flows, my actual body, spirit, and mind need to live these seasons as well. It is as if a part of me is the art and I need to go through the cycle with it. After all, the art and the creative act that births it is not separate from the artist's own self.

Living these truths inherent in the flow of creation can be difficult in a world that is always "on." We face tremendous pressure to always be generating noise. But it is a myth to think life is only going well when we're constantly using our gifts and accomplishing great things. We don't need much encouragement about the value of heightened peaks of outward achievement—our society affirms this in spades. What we sorely need is to remind ourselves that the quieter seasons have validity, too. It is the dormant times that allow space in our own lives for perspective and recalibration for the next chapter. When this space isn't allowed for, the results tend to be off kilter, much in the same way that a scientific device that isn't calibrated won't function correctly, or a musical instrument that isn't tuned won't sound harmonious. It is in dormant times that we allow our very selves to be tuned to the frequency of the next chapter in life.

JRR Tolkien famously said, "Not all those who wander are lost." We must take this to heart along the way in our artist journey. The in-between times are indeed a valuable part of life as well. The reassuring truth is that the next thing will come; it always does. When dormancy appears on our step, it behooves us to embrace it and acknowledge the whole rhythm of life, both for the good of our own souls and for the good of our art. What we create next will emerge from a root system that has been given time to grow wide and deep.

— ELEVEN —
Spirituality and Art

For me, art is a spiritual practice first and foremost. Ultimately, I think this not only helps preserve creativity, but allows it to really flourish. This is what I want when I create. This is why I create, actually. When art is reduced to merely a product or an occupation, or something only definable with clear parameters and boundaries, it loses a tremendous amount of capacity to impact. Something that has infinite energetic potential is turned into a shell of its fully expressed self. Despite the fact that the creative work may be extremely well-crafted, the soul is missing. There is an emptiness to art with no soul. Even if not easily explained, this sort of sterility can usually be sensed and felt.

I think many artists know this innately and learn how to tap into something larger than themselves as they create. Initially, it can be very easy to just make art from an intellectual understanding of color, composition, or some other learned principle. But the creative process becomes infinitely more liberating and freeing when it starts to transcend the limits of our minds. In my own process, I've found spiritual meaning often appears in what I have created long after I have finished creating it, whether in the form of a higher truth about my own life or something relevant for the world at large. These insights are never something I'm aware of before I begin.

When I first noticed this extra layer of expansion in my art practice, it was like discovering a fascinating surprise factor thrown into the creative process. These a-ha moments of meaning were really quite timely and often prophetic in nature. To me, this is what makes the act of creation truly magical. I think art making allows us to experience an act of divinity, whether we have a logical belief in something divine or not. We act as a conduit for an energy flow that comes from outside of ourselves.

It can be quite easy to forget about this side of life, especially in a western world that tends to elevate the rational mind above the intuitive one. A spiritual creative practice, however, is a direct path to the intuitive mind and is an incredibly powerful way of knowing. Becoming connected to this way of knowing is especially important for artists, as there is a direct connection between what goes on in one's soul and the artistic expression that pours forth (for better or for worse). Engaging with creativity in this elevated form is almost akin to a dance between the soul and the universe, a mutually edifying back and forth exchange. The very process of engaging with your creative gifts in this way becomes replenishing in and of itself, because it becomes a source of life, of nourishment.

This is true not only for the one doing the creating, but for the audience as well. Art made from this place tends to bypass the mind and penetrate people's hearts. I think this is what makes it so powerful. The way we "see" art isn't just a surface level seeing, but it is something that penetrates a deeper layer within. We register the very substance or energy of what we are seeing. Our minds and their logical reasoning often keep us blinded to an awareness of this spiritual side of life. So creative expressions that speak to this part of ourselves, instead of directly to the mind, can help facilitate and deepen our awareness. The viewer is left with an experience of something sacred.

Tapping into this force, then, becomes powerful both for one's own creative flow and sense of synchronicity and also for the rest of society. Art in all forms that is birthed from a higher place will contribute something beneficial to the world. In this sense, artists have the ability to wield a tremendous amount of power. Every noble cause on the planet must eventually necessitate a move from "I" to "we." So learning to create from a spiritual plane makes art not merely a personal expression, but an entity with a much larger and collective life force, an entity that, in turn, can exert much positive influence upon the world.

I've seen this reality in action many times in my own art practice over the years. As I already mentioned, I first experienced this on a personal level when I began creating small works of art in my home studio. But I didn't really see the full impact that art could have on shifting energy and impacting others until I entered the public art realm. It was there that I observed the power creative expressions have to change the surrounding environment.

My first experience of observing the public's reaction to something I created in front of them took place at the complex where I rented my first studio. There was a large sliding door at the entrance to my space, and one day I decided to create a collage on the front of it. This was the first time I'd created art in front of other people. In this case, it was just people passing by in the hallway, but nevertheless, it was a shift for me from the privacy of creating alone in my studio.

What was significant about this experience for me was that I was still creating from a place of spirit, but this time, because it was in public, I could see the effect that it had on others. People's demeanor changed as they walked by and were drawn to what was being created. It seemed to lift their spirits and release something positive. It became obvious to me that my work was somehow shifting the climate. And the thing is, I felt like I was an observer in much the same way everyone else was. I was letting my hands be used to create something, but consciously I wasn't directing the flow of it. I was a participant in a larger process that was unfolding.

Later on, after finishing, awareness came to me that the title of what I'd created was *Tree of Life* (which I later changed to *Healing Leaves*), because rejuvenation was what the collaged papers appeared to release energetically. Months later, a friend of mine, whom I had not shared this experience with, attended an open studio event and saw my door for the first time. She said to me that as she walked by, she heard in her spirit the words "tree of life." Given that what I'd made was an abstract creation and did not look like an obvious or literal tree, and that I had told her nothing about this particular collage or what it was called, her experience served to affirm my participation in a larger act of creation that went far beyond me and my own human understanding.

About a year and a half after this incident, I painted my

first public mural. This gave me a front row seat in observing just how powerful art can be when it shifts from just a personal expression to a larger life force. I was constantly amazed at how people lit up as they walked by the wall where I was painting, so interested in what was happening and excited by it. One homeless man, whom I found camped out underneath the mural one morning, told me that he was resting there because of the good energy he felt coming from the wall. Another man, who worked in the car repair shop adjacent to the building, was initially grumpy and unfriendly when I first introduced myself to him. But over the course of the project, his demeanor slowly changed, and one day he came out and said to me with a huge smile, "Thank you for the music!", referring to his experience of the painting that had been growing each week.

People who had previously not paid attention to this particular street corner started coming by regularly to check on my progress. Several even brought me gifts, like cold drinks, a sweater on a chilly evening, a brush cleaner, etc. What sparked this kind of generosity, this connection with random strangers on the street? The power of a higher energy flow did. People regularly communicated that they felt peace and calm radiating from the painting and they expressed joy that it was serving to brighten up the neighborhood.

Observing what my creation is radiating is a key to knowing whether I've partnered with a higher life force or simply created out of my own ego. Contrary to the stereotype of artists creating from their own angst, creating when you are anchored by a larger spiritual force results in an experience of inner and outer tranquility.

Pauliina Haustein, a cellist, describes her experience of this partnership as "stepping into a river, a flow, where I can feel things coming together with greater ease and impacting those around me. My spirit rises above the technical challenges of playing and the river carries me. It is the ultimate moment of creativity, of being carried and embraced by its flow." At these peaks, creativity becomes a place of true union.

I love this quote by authors Rosamund and Benjamin Zander, as it describes so well the spiritual impact works of art can have upon the world: "Art, after all, is about rearranging us, creating surprising juxtapositions, emotional openings, startling presences, flight paths to the eternal." Using art as a tool to create pathways to the eternal is appealing to me on a very deep level. It is a way of participating in the world's transformation. It is a way of taking creative gifts and elevating them to their highest possible potential.

— TWELVE —

Listening and Being Comfortable with the Unknown

So how do we tap in to this spiritual side of art? How do we let our art be of ultimate service to others in this way? I think the best way to be a conduit in this manner is to listen. Learning how to do this is key. Because "spiritual" simply means we're connecting to something larger than ourselves. But to do that, to really listen, we need to incorporate stillness into our lives so that we have space to hear any messages that are trying to come through.

The creative voice usually comes as a quiet voice. It doesn't come shouting for attention. We can easily miss it in the clamor of other thoughts and voices that present themselves, almost always with a greater sense of urgency and immediacy. In this regard, stillness is something we must actively fight for. Hearing the voice itself and letting it take root as something that must be born is the beginning of this process. Whether it be a seed of an idea, an inspired image, or the beginning of a story, we won't be able to hear if we don't pay attention and if we don't take initiative to designate space for it to emerge.

Inner stillness is a rare commodity in this day and age, which is all the more reason that it is valuable to cultivate. Being still allows us to create in the present moment. When we can settle into this quiet place, we have the best chance of being able to listen to each piece and let it chart its own course. Allowing this process fosters greater creative growth and potential. It gives permission for creativity to come from a deeper place within.

Listening in an atmosphere of stillness also provides the artist with a great freedom. It allows him or her to let the creation be what it is and offers liberation from the compulsion to overwork it or try to make it into something that it is not. It aids synchronicity.

I learned this lesson repeatedly when I began mural painting. The first project I tackled, which I mentioned in the last chapter, wasn't mapped out on the wall before beginning, so the whole process of creating it was an exercise in listening and in not turning the mural into something that was solely limited to my own understanding. Trusting that it would tell me what it was meant to be and that my only job was to paint it was not always easy. Some days I was able to enter into this flow and go with it and feel quite liberated, and other days my analytical brain took over and forgot about connecting to the larger life force that was there to support me. But despite the challenges, I found that tapping into a place of inner stillness for guidance helped me get in sync with the instincts that wanted to flow.

I've been practicing listening and stillness as I write this book. When I began, my first step was to dig through a copious amount of old writing...all my old blog posts, journal entries, snippets of writing on my laptop, and so forth. I had the sense inside of me that at the very least, a skeleton of a book on creativity might already be contained in the entirety of my writings from the past several years, and so I needed to comb through all of it in order to find that beginning structure.

The key to sorting through everything was to simply just listen as I reread old excerpts and ask, *Is this something that wants to be in the book?* As I began to sort and compile material in this manner, my main task was to just observe what was forming in front of me and then, from there, gain a clearer sense of direction as to what the book was meant to be.

Listening to the overall voice the book wanted to have was really helpful, because logically, it could have been many things...the journey that led me to become an artist, a more philosophical survey of art and its role in society, a "how-to" book for making art, a self-help guide, a book looking at deeper principles that guide the creative journey (which is where I landed), and so forth. I needed to listen to hear the voice that was already coming through on its own, and then reorient myself to get in sync with it and support what wanted to come out. Julia Cameron once said that if the work comes to the artist and says, "Here I am, serve me," then the job of the artist, great or small, is to serve.

As we do this, we are always led to the place we need to go next, even if the direction doesn't initially make sense. A few years ago I wrote this sentiment on my blog, which describes very well the contrast between a less defined and at times unknown road and a straight, clearly prescribed one: "Sometimes the path through life is winding and offers up untrodden twists and turns that hint at adventure and spark curiosity. It asks for a willingness to surrender to the unknown, to trust the turns without being able to see what's ahead, and to delight in the myriad of discoveries that are within reach with each step. An explorer's path. And quite often, it seems, right next to this wooded trail of the unknown is a concrete highway laid bare, a multitude of cars whizzing by in a well-defined straight line. Because this route is well-traversed and firmly delineated, the drivers need not pay attention to their immediate surroundings nor even to which way to head their racing vehicles. Observations of the surrounding environment are lost as speed and arriving at the end of the road take precedence. As I stand hesitantly between freeway and wooded glen, it is the winding path that seems to be beckoning. I glance over my shoulder and feel a seed of doubt. A nearby bird chirps on the leafy trail and flutters a few steps ahead. It is the winding path I will take, with open hands and an expectation of discovery."

As artists, if we are truly going to listen and take action with what we hear, a winding path is par for the course. Creativity will always lead us past the road that is clearly defined. A certain amount of faith becomes a prerequisite. Because creativity has a high level of mysticism, one must absolutely be able to embrace the unknown. The good news is, a large part of the joy of creating *is* the unknown. As opposed to being something to fear or correct or control, it is instead an invitation to a child's game of exploration, of trusting that the next thing will come, of learning to be present to what is forming right now in this moment and not needing to see five steps down the road.

This can feel counterintuitive in many ways, especially

since we've been trained in linear thinking and having clearly delineated steps for achieving goals. Much of this kind of thinking needs to be suspended from time to time in a creative practice that is centered on listening. Many times preconceived ideas about the kind of art I'm going to make or how a particular piece is going to turn out must be surrendered so that something new, perhaps something entirely different than anything I may have imagined, can come forth.

I have found letting go of the need to know incredibly freeing. Trying to know and figure out things that really can't be known ahead of time can be a cumbersome burden and result in much fruitless work. Letting go of knowing helps us surrender to flow. It is paradoxically a gateway into that bliss state of creating, where you are unaware of time passing and can hear inner directives clearly and easily.

Not knowing is especially an asset in the blocked times and in the waiting times, in seasons when all direction and sense of passion are gone. During these times, life forces you to journey far deeper into the realm of not knowing than you ever willingly want to go. But this too, is a gift of art. It regularly requires giving up knowing "the plan."

Very simply, the act of creation is not a straight line path. And that's ok. In this sense, it is actually a far more magical road to travel. It is full of synchronicity and unexpected discoveries. It requires trust and an ability to see life through a lens of mystery. It regularly asks for surrender, which always leads us to a larger place than we ever could have imagined on our own. In a way, it serves to free us from the limits of linear thinking and opens up a larger world of possibility.

The truth is, we can't fully imagine the extent of what we can become with our own limited thinking. Sure, we can dream and have big ideas and move towards exciting goals, but in order to realize our greatest potential, we need the mind of something infinite. It is with this sense of the infinite that we partner to grow into the fullness of our true selves. This reality is often hidden from the logic of our human minds and our finite knowing. So being willing to live in the unknown is actually a tool around this block, and ends up being an incredibly expansive and powerful place to be!

The unknown will always serve to expand us, because it is by nature an expansive energy. It is in this place that we drop old constructs and limited thinking and start to recognize an infinite force beyond ourselves that seeks to partner with us to achieve our highest potential. We move into the realm of possibility. We are freed to embrace uncertainty, to believe that it will be figured out as we go along, to know that beginning is the most important thing, and to have faith that ultimately each step thereafter will result in a more expansive outcome than we would ever have been able to anticipate otherwise. It is in listening and welcoming the unknown that we are led to create from a place of partnership and trust.

—THIRTEEN—

Replenishing the Well

At its deepest level, creating art is an act of the soul. For this to be true, this same soul must be guarded and nourished, as this kind of focused engagement requires our entire being.

Art emerges from the very depths of ourselves. It requires pouring out what is within. And so we have no choice but to pay attention to these inner places and monitor their well-being. Our creative wells must be replenished on a regular basis, otherwise, impetus falters and we can easily lose the wonder of creating.

When we're exhausted or burned out, reigniting the flame of joy in our lives regenerates our momentum. Even though I have learned this time and time again, it amazes me how much I still resist taking time for replenishing my own creative well. It is far too easy to give in to the predominant cultural voice that emphasizes production and busyness above all else. This mentality is a big hindrance to the arts and their development, and to their quality as well.

It is from places of refreshment and times of play

that I receive creative inspiration and direction. And of course, any activity that serves to inspire and rejuvenate ends up becoming a significant aid to future production—it enhances quality and depth of creative expression like nothing else.

When you skip replenishing your spirit and just move into a rote mode of creating, you get disconnected from your center and from the very origin of your creative flow. You forget that nurture is actually a pathway to creative fruit. You forget the counter-intuitive wisdom that play and pleasure are fuel for creativity. It becomes necessary then, as artists, to follow a countercultural voice to stoke the coals of our creative fires. We must remember that creative work is not always outward in direction. Taking time to replenish the spirit allows us to tap into and create from a deep inner well of life.

For me, replenishing this well happens most deeply and most easily when I am in nature. Living by the ocean provides me with an automatic outlet for recharging. Water has a way of leaving me feeling refreshed every time I am near it. The sound of the waves, the vast horizon line, the smell of salt in the air, watching seagulls in flight overhead...all these things are like deposits for my creative center. So is time spent in the surrounding hills, enjoying the peace and quiet of trees, flowers in bloom, and winding trails. Time away in nature inevitably changes me. It changes the very place from which I create.

The difference for me when I allow for this replenishing is like night and day. When I return to my studio, I have something to offer the world again. Vital creative energy is released. Experiences of beauty affect me in much the same way. I've learned that I need to take in beauty regularly if I am going to create beauty. Art is very much a two-way street in this respect. So, I've become a regular beauty seeker and appreciator. Things like the sound of running water from a fountain, brightly colored tile work on my walk, a well-written and thought-provoking book, a colorful mural leading to the ocean, the sound of my neighbor playing the piano...these are all experiences of beauty for me. The visual or mental stimulation that results is so helpful for keeping things fresh and my work inspired.

Seeking out these experiences doesn't have to be difficult, costly, or time consuming. The most pleasurable things are often the most profound in their simplicity. But they must be given space to enter our spirit. That is really the key, I think. This is the ultimate challenge in our over-worked and over-stimulated culture. We don't take time to see or take in the small pleasures of life. We are even at a loss as to how to do this when we do have time. Many of us have lost the ability to be present to the present moment. We are too busy ignoring the state of our inner being, which comes at great cost to ourselves and to the world around us.

My artist friend Shari wrote this observation about the creative path: "If I didn't appreciate it before, I have learned just how closely intertwined my creativity and inner life are. Robustness in one proves hopelessly impossible without the same in the other." This sentiment is full of resonance for me. It reconnects me to my own desire to be a whole person and to pay attention to all facets of my life as I create.

You cannot fully thrive in the outer arena of the creative life without a vibrant inner center. In fact, I would say it is exceedingly difficult to create when one's inner life is not in a good place. Creating requires energy from an inner life source. And if this life source is non-existent, dim, or faltering, creativity becomes that much harder to release and sometimes gets blocked all together.

So we can't ignore prompts to care for our soul. This is directly connected to what we make. It is not self-indulgent to do this; it is necessary. Otherwise, it's too easy to slip back into letting society dictate who we become, to our detriment, with its almost constant emphasis on external outcomes and lack of attention to anything internal.

The creative path is a lot of pushing out, of repeatedly making and finding your own opportunities, and continually crafting new bodies of work. It is primarily about creating something from nothing over and over again. Day after day, when your life's work is driven solely by you, replenishing becomes all the more a vital part of the cycle.

On a recent morning, I felt prompted to spend time looking at a coffee table book I had recently purchased at Nepenthe Cafe in Big Sur (for those of you who don't know, Nepenthe has historically been a gathering place for artists, writers, and other creatives along the central California coastline). This book was attractive to me because it was full of color and illustrations and an interesting written account of Kaffe Fassett's life, an artist who inspired me. He is the son of the couple who built Nepenthe and grew up amongst an eclectic group of artists, all living a myriad of creative vocations along the Big Sur coastline.

Normally I begin writing first thing every morning, but on this day I felt a prompt to pick up this particular book and enjoy it a bit before I began my morning writing session. I'd been putting off looking at it until I "had time," but that time had yet to appear. I knew that even perusing it just a bit would be like a drink for my soul. So when the prompt came "Take this in before you pour yourself out," I listened. And I saw so much of myself in this particular artist's writings and his description of his creative journey, it only served to affirm and encourage me to keep going on mine.

The daily discipline of an art or writing practice can easily falter and doesn't receive much support or affirmation from the outside world. Reading about Fassett's life and the strength of his own inner compass, which is what kept propelling him forward, gave me needed juice for continuing my own work. It helped me dive into my own writing that morning with greater resolve and with a greater belief in the creativity I had to offer the world. It allowed me to resume my work with a full cup, able to pour out what I had just been given.

Life, with a capital L, comes knocking on our door every day. It is set before us in daily, recognizable ways. This is the reality of an abundant universe. As we learn to recognize this abundance and allow ourselves to receive it, we are much better equipped for the creative work that lies before us. We have something fresh to offer. A sustainable creative practice is supported by seeing with renewed eyes the refreshment that is available if we would but choose to partake. The trick is just reminding ourselves to say yes.

During a recent drive back down the coast from Northern California, I chose to say yes to the majestic views that were beyond a doubt an indelible reflection of this abundant universe. I stopped the car to take time to savor them, and, like a drink for my entire being, they reminded me of the vastness, wildness and beauty of the natural world and how much of it is beyond our limited understanding. I was reminded that I am part of this incredible greatness flung across the earth, and so could trust once more that I was being given exactly what I needed.

Awareness of our participation in this flow serves to loosen our grip on life. We are grounded again to move forward in peace instead of from a place of lack. With gratitude, I left that vista feeling renewed and moving forward with a full cup, not an empty one. I left energized to once again take up my calling to release the gift of creativity into the world.

―FOURTEEN―

Remembering That Artists Are Changemakers

I think creatives are, by nature, meant to live outside of boxes. To birth something into existence that has never been created before requires seeing the world around you differently. This unique outlook is an asset in many ways, to you and also to those around you and to the larger community, because it serves as a needed voice in a world that too often encourages conformity and sameness. Anyone who is able to carve a different path than the one dictated by the predominant culture demonstrates that you don't necessarily have to live life adhering to one script. Being trapped in a rut is not an unchangeable reality.

By choosing to not confine themselves to a pre-scripted path, artists challenge limited thinking and bring expansion and newness. In this way, we are true change makers. We have the capacity to catapult ourselves outside of everyday sameness and routine, and we serve as a reminder to the rest of society that you can create a new track if you don't like the one you're on.

Artists and our creations remind us of what is possible. They remind us to dream. By taking an unscripted view of life, artists model the truth that we do have choices about how we live, more than we may think. Old and dusty trails can be left behind for fresh ones. Our lives can indeed evolve and grow and take on new dimensions. Artists enable us to see what we couldn't see before, and in doing so, expand our paradigms and broaden our understanding of how the world works.

I know quite a bit about scripted living and sameness and routine, as I grew up in a region of the country that emphasized conformity and a one-track mindset. One of the benefits that I've enjoyed then, working as an artist in Los Angeles, is the city's emphasis on foregoing tradition. I think this helps the arts and innovation tremendously. It helps cultivate a "change-making" ethos.

Creativity thrives in an outside-of-the-box environment. The further outside of the box that artists roam, the more inventive their creations become. Los Angeles is an ideal place for this kind of experimentation. There is something in the culture here that encourages being different and celebrates trying without fear of failure. In LA, the prevailing mindset would say that it is better to have at least tried to manifest your destiny than to not have attempted it at all. This kind of thinking is an incredible boon to the arts and their development.

I was reminded of this recently as I was reading an excerpt from a press release for an upcoming exhibit highlighting the work of London artists living in LA. The press release stated: "The move to LA has encouraged an evolution, even a revolution, in the creation of their work. It is well known that artists such as David Hockney blazed a trail for expats who, like him, moved west to experience the openness, the newness...of Southern California. Freed from the artistic traditions and institutions of older cities, the blue-sky creative climate in LA and its continually developing art scene have allowed for a fresh perspective for expat artists."

I think artists of all stripes are drawn to living in areas that buck convention because of the creative freedom these places embody. This sense of freedom in LA has certainly fostered my own development and growth in amazing ways. Unconventional thinking and permission to roam outside of boxes energizes me creatively. I have found that when I have taken a risk to pursue sheer creative desire, even when it didn't initially make sense, it has always paid off and led me to something beneficial. Working in a climate where there are no felt restrictions on what can be imagined is a huge gift. It allows me to embrace fully the trailblazing nature of art. And it assists all artist change makers who are looking for the path that doesn't yet exist, instead of acquiescing to the one that has already been cut and laid out.

It is natural for artists to begin their careers thinking in very inventive ways, giving full leash to their inquisitiveness and ability to think outside of normal guidelines. But slowly, over time, the box of artistic "success" can creep in, and a narrow road starts to appear that can easily feel limiting. It is all too easy to lose our art in search of our career. We can easily forget that we are the ones who create meaning with our art, and we can lose touch with the roots of authenticity. We can look too much to the world's system to define how we do art and what direction we take with it, to the point of letting creativity become a rote, almost empty exercise.

I've seen many artists achieve an admirable level of commercial success but still lose the will to create. I've seen many give up creating all together. Even though they had the accolades that the art world uses to define success, to me, they lost what was most important and sacred: the purity of beginnings. They lost creative integrity. They lost creative joy.

The institutionalization of art and the one-track mindset of the system can inadvertently make you forget who you are as an artist. It can cause you to lose touch with that inner knowing, that inner flow from which creativity is birthed. Like all systems, the system of art wants to label things and categorize them and pass judgments. And if these methods of categorizing stop serving as teaching elements (which they can be initially) and just become noise, then we are no longer able to hear that small voice inside, that prompt. *These words. That color. This shape.* Too much noise from the art world can make it very hard to hear and we can get steered off course.

Sometimes it is not the noise but the uber seriousness of the prestigious, higher ends of the art world that can leave the artist feeling more trapped and less free than before he or she started creating. We need the reminder to periodically throw out all the conventions and rules that we or others have put on the creative process along the way and think outside of their framework again.

A child's spirit exhibits true freedom. And in its most pure form, art is an amazing tool that helps adults excavate a childlike spirit that has been covered over by years of living. This means a less than perfect craft from time to time. This means exploration. This means trying new things that may or may not succeed. Imperfection and taking a break from the linear thinking of a traditional artist career path aids experimentation. If we lose the ability to do this, then we diminish the possibility of art being truly unique and reaching its fullest potential as an agent of change.

Art is a mechanism, but like all mechanisms, it is meant to serve us and not the other way around. We must be careful that we don't become enslaved to the mechanism and start meeting its demands instead of those of a larger purpose. For me, the writing of this book coincided with letting go of the art I "should" be making to continue my career, and returning to a place of freedom with a new series of small drawings that had absolutely nothing to do visually with anything I'd been creating or building for my portfolio the past several years. However, I knew instinctually that these small drawings were somehow intricately connected to the writing process of the book. The energy of one was going to feed the other.

It became apparent that they were joint projects, so to speak, whose births were dependent on each other. So in this sense, it was quite necessary to follow this new direction. In many ways, this felt tremendously liberating, but it also set off a few internal panic buttons. Thoughts like, *But I'm known for a certain kind of art and this isn't it,* or *Book art installations are what I've been building my portfolio around,* etc., all flowed through my head. Over time, I came to see how the new art I was making was mirroring and supporting the writing I was doing in ways I could never have anticipated. Each drawing was illustrating a facet of the writer identity that was being formed within me.

There have been other times as well that I've ventured into new territory as an artist and tried things I'd never done before, all to the dismay of the straight lines that wanted to set themselves around my art practice. But if you can't change your path as an artist, then what good is the path? If there is any occupation that should be able to shift and morph and evolve, it is the creative one. The foundation of a creative life is self-expression. But our "selves" do not remain static throughout life. So why should our art?

I think part of maintaining our role as change makers in society involves remembering that arriving is a myth. This truth is both uncomfortable and freeing at the same time. The reality is there is always more to explore, more to learn, and more to grow and become. But the problem is, we all too often want to arrive. Arrival gives us a sense of security and control. A sense of accomplishment. But as artists, we must be willing to explore new avenues and let go of what is familiar and safe. That is what creativity is about. We have to let our creations morph into something new, if and when that is called for.

When we purposely resist change, we can easily grow stagnant and cautious. We also run the risk of becoming stuck. When we give into the idea that we have arrived, we are then faced with the temptation to cease growing. If innovation is at the heart of great art and is what spurs needed cultural shifts in society, then all the more reason to be willing to let go of a routine that has gone stale. I don't know many artists who have established themselves successfully with a certain body of work who don't feel at least a small seed of trepidation at leaving this set platform for the sake of something new. Especially when the system of art, in the form of gallery or collector expectations, is not always supportive of or responsive to a new direction. But I think as artists, we at least must be willing to entertain this idea from time to time. We must create with an open enough mind to allow a new thing to be born, if that is what the muse calls for.

Permission is key to embracing a change-making role. We must remember to give ourselves permission to follow whatever the unique expression is that is ours to claim. I struggled with permission when I began to think about painting murals and entering the public art realm. Public art wasn't something that fit with the genre of art I'd been making. It didn't fit with the career goal of building a resume of gallery exhibits. It certainly wasn't a guaranteed money maker. But I knew that it was something I needed to do, not just for me, but for the benefit of the public. In some ways, public art is a much more effective change-making agent in the larger culture than anything in a gallery setting, mostly because it is so much more visible and accessible to the public eye.

I was fortunate to meet an artist in Los Angeles named Evan Meyer who began a grassroots mural painting movement in Santa Monica. It is through his organization that I was first introduced to public art and was able to witness firsthand how it can literally alter a neighborhood. He is one of the most effective change-making artists I know, and he has created an entire movement around art that has produced significant, lasting change in numerous communities. He is an expert at operating outside of preconceived expectations of what art must be.

Creative impulses that start movements like this can get easily buried by the stuff of life: roles, finances, others' expectations, practicality, the norms of an official art career, etc. But permission returns us to the place of creative beginnings where anything is possible, where there are no restraints, no market that demands one product, no gallery to please. Just the spirit of creativity flowing through you. Guarding this sacred place is perhaps one of the marks of true success in a creative career, in my mind. Can we stay true to the roots of our creative selves in the midst of a career that tends to move us away from them? Can we manage to maintain that flow, that innocence and purity with which we began? I think this is key to letting our art be a potent force for changing society.

Art by its very nature is not meant to be defined by strict rules or to mirror a script that is pleasing to society. And at the end of the day, much of carving a trail blazing path in the arts over the long-term is simply about returning. We all lose our way at some point in the venture. Ups and downs are to be expected as we navigate external forces that don't always celebrate inventiveness and as we learn to figure out our own steps, bit by bit.

But the good news is that it's not so much about not losing your way as it is about remembering to return once you've lost your bearings. We remember our origins. We recover and nourish the creative root that fueled us in the first place. We remember that we haven't arrived and that there is permission for something new. It is in the act of returning that we spot the thread again. And even though we might not know where the thread is leading next, the simple act of picking it up once more and taking a step forward brings us outside the box to begin our trail blazing anew.

—FIFTEEN—
Redemption in Life Calling

I'd like to include this last chapter as a place of hope and encouragement for anyone reading this book, as a reminder that no matter one's life calling, the work we do with our hands has the potential to reconcile things from our past and change us in the present. Given that we spend most of our lives doing some type of work, shouldn't it be something that aids in our own transformation? Work need not be just meaningless labor, solely for scraping together enough dollars to live out the lives we've chosen. Surely as humans we have higher possibility than that. Surely a piece of what is at stake is our potential to evolve and transcend a bit of the earthly realm we're relegated to during our short years on the planet. No matter what work we do, we have the possibility of expanding through it, if we are able to choose this perspective. When we allow for this, any work we put our hands to has the capacity to become a tool for change in our lives.

I've pondered many times over the past several years how art is a great tool of change in my own life. It seems to have a considerable knack for teaching me the exact things I need to be learning. Sometimes I forget this, as it is easy to respond with resistance to obstacles or difficulties that come with creative pursuits.

But the reality is, freedom often comes from the things we resist if we are able to embrace them. If we can move past our resistance and allow challenges to be integrated into who we are, we can be led into a place of greater liberation. I have seen this happen in many ways in my life over the last decade of art making.

I mentioned in the introduction to this book that one of the initial challenges for me in pursuing an art career was becoming comfortable with visibility. In many ways my creative work, both art and now writing, has been hugely instrumental in my journey of learning to value visibility and discover a sense of self. This is significant for me because I have not always been visible or had an identifiable voice that was my own. Historically, I have been the one to listen quietly as others speak, to offer understanding and affirmation of others' insights, but to keep my own locked up inside.

My tendency to lose my sense of self in the presence of others came partially from having functioned in a caregiving capacity in different ways during my growing up years, and also as a result of gender conditioning. Society routinely steers women to think first and foremost about the world around them, often to the exclusion of self. Another piece of it came from having grown up in a religious culture that further emphasized a denial of the self and putting others' needs first.

My conscientious nature interpreted the entirety of these influences to mean carrying the weight of the world on my shoulders. My voice was obscured for years by an overdeveloped awareness of everyone else's sense of self and their accompanying needs. Helping others took the place of internal development of my own identity—so much so, that despite a myriad of creative interests as a child, pursuing a career in social work was the only thing that made sense to me in my young adult years. I had very little awareness of my own self and an outsized awareness of others.

The irony, of course, is that you can't really give away something you haven't found in the first place. You can't be of service to others fully until you have a developed sense of self to give away. Someone once said that art is the fiercest form of individualism the world has ever known. I would say this rings true in the sense that art forces you to find yourself in order to express it. And that was exactly what I needed. However, years of prioritizing the needs of the outside world made it very hard to initially identify what my own contribution was. So the process of discovering my own voice through the arts and beginning to express it was hugely significant. Learning to find and articulate it required a tremendous amount of work on my part. It forced me to go within and discover the self that was waiting there all along.

But art pushed me one step beyond just discovering the self and expressing it—it pushed me to move to the level of influence. It taught me to recognize that creative expressions serve to shape the world around me. And it was my job to exert influence in this way. For someone who had historically stayed in the shadows while helping others, this initially felt quite scary and daunting.

But as is true for all of us, growth is usually manageable

when approached in small steps. And so small steps are what I took. A discovery of an artist identity led to a beginning doodle, which led to an exploration of collage, which then progressed to larger works of art and then to public art, and then ultimately to writing words on a page for people to digest and ponder. This journey reflects a self that has not only been found, but that has grown braver over the years, in both ability to express and willingness to be seen. It reflects a self that has chosen to become an influencer by producing works of art and writing that serve to challenge and uplift others for the betterment of society.

Staying hidden would have been the easier path for me by far, the one that required less effort and far less risk and personal growth. But as an artist, learning to express my voice was essential; there really wasn't an option not to. The creative voice is the only tool artists have for impacting the world. In that sense, self-expression became not only a conduit for personal growth and a redemption of my past self, but it also became a gift to offer others.

One of the most freeing things I've learned along the way is that people's response to my visibility isn't what matters. In a way, I start with an advantage in this respect, in the sense that I don't have an innate desire for fame or amassing a huge following. Not that I am against any of that, but those accolades do not drive me. This frees me from giving any kind of excessive weight to external opinions.

What does drive me is a belief both in the value of what I have to offer and in the positive effect it can have on the world. This is what is meaningful. So, spending energy on detractors becomes a waste of time. Letting fear control us and giving into worry about what other people think or how they will respond is all wasted energy. What truly matters is discovering your voice and your contribution and then making it. Committing to the work involved is what is important; the particular kind of impact it has isn't in our control.

This is tremendously liberating for an artist, because then we don't have to fear following a gut impulse or taking a risk with a new form of expression. If we let go of others' responses and focus instead on doing the work to express what is coming through us, the voice is liberated to be what it is meant to be.

There are many ways in which the nature of art, namely the ebb and flow of the creative cycle, aids me in needed personal growth. It has taught me in a new way to allow for process. Creative work is much more about letting things unfold then about forcing them to happen. It is equal parts internal incubation and external expression.

Many artists I know live with this natural ebb and flow more easily than I do. I am one who has always liked the idea of constant growth and constant forward movement (or at least the illusion of constant). But not only is this not realistic, it is certainly not what I need. I actually need to allow the ebb and flow of the cycle for the sake of my soul's health and evolution. The timeline of gestation and birth for each creative project can vary wildly and much important creative work happens internally, long before anything external comes into being.

In this way, the process of making art is a needed force for my own growth. It has taught me that you don't always need an external focus and you don't always need speed. These are two lies propagated quite readily by Western culture, and I can fall prey to both of them fairly easily.

But the reality is, this over-fixation on external results and speed often robs my soul of contentment.

And so the gift of the artist path for me is learning to welcome the internal work that is involved and to occasionally put on hold my desire for external outcomes and my need to have them happen now. Art teaches me to be in the present moment. This curbs my spirit's tendency to be anxious about getting to the next thing. Over years of art making, I have learned to be at peace with the daily, incremental progress of the work. Whereas early on in my career I would resist the slow times I encountered, I now more easily welcome these periods because I realize that they teach me how to take a side road. Traversing the entirety of the creative path teaches me to live with greater balance.

Ultimately, I think our passions in life have the capacity to lead us to the kind of work we really need to be doing for our own growth. This is still true, even and especially in seasons of our creative work that may be more mundane than inspired. If we are open to the mindset of growth, we have the capacity to receive an entirely new layer of meaning around what we do. When we take a larger-picture view of our lives, we can believe that there is purpose being worked out in our daily movement. Believing there is some kind of redeeming value in the creative work we are called to do means believing in the possibility of our lives being expanded and transformed. It means choosing to trust that there is no wasted effort. It means having faith that our creative practice and our lives are indeed being worked out in the manner best suited to our own evolution.

About the Author

Karen Kinney is a mixed media artist professionally affiliated with the Los Angeles Art Association and The Center for Book Arts in New York. Her work has been in numerous solo, group, and juried exhibitions, both nationally and internationally. Her art was purchased for the Lionsgate film *The Lincoln Lawyer* and resides in private collections across the country, including those of actor Bob Odenkirk and NPR's Guy Raz.

She likes to use a variety of materials as she creates. Her work often begins with a paint stroke, a shred of paper, or some ink scratches on pages taken from old books. The use of vibrant colors is important to her, as it contributes to the feeling of something new emerging from what has been discarded. In addition to small-scale collages, she also creates large installations and is currently building a temporary installation for the Los Angeles International Airport.

In recent years she has become a strong advocate of public art and continues to seek out opportunities to beautify communities through mural painting. She lives in Los Angeles with her husband.

KarenKinney.com
Twitter: @karen_e_kinney
Instagram: @karen_e_kinney
Facebook.com/karen.kinney.4

www.ingramcontent.com/pod-product-compliance
Lightning Source LLC
Chambersburg PA
CBHW020258030426
42336CB00010B/833